G000256391

My England

My England

Impression for Young Readers

by

RICHARD CHURCH
PAULINE CLARKE
HELEN CRESSWELL
LEON GARFIELD
JACYNTH HOPE-SIMPSON
PENELOPE LIVELY
ELFRIDA VIPONT

Illustrated by
ANTHONY COLBERT

HEINEMANN : LONDON

William Heinemann Ltd
15 Queen St, Mayfair, London W1X 8BE
LONDON MELBOURNE TORONTO
JOHANNESBURG AUCKLAND

First published 1973

SBN 434 93256 6

Filmset and printed in England by
Cox & Wyman Ltd, London, Fakenham and Reading

Contents

LAND'S END

by Jacynth Hope-Simpson

Cornwall and England face one another across the water.

It is usually easy to pass from one English county to another. The road winds on, with nothing to mark the change, except for a small metal plaque on the grass verge. Cornwall is different. Three sides of the county are entirely surrounded by sea. On the fourth flows the River Tamar. It rises only four miles from the Atlantic coast in the north, and flows south to the English Channel. As the river grows wider, it cuts the southwestern peninsula into two. It flows between cliff-like, tree-covered banks, and through marshes haunted by birds. For thousands of years the only way of crossing the lower

Tamar was to take a boat over its tidal waters, and, frequently, to get soaked to the skin in the process.

Few people troubled to do so. The Romans built no important settlements there. All through the Middle Ages, that great age of church building, Cornwall had no cathedral. Later, no powerful landowner wished to live there, so far from the centre of things. Cornwall has never had a great house like Longleat, Woburn, or Blenheim. There was nobody but the Cornish themselves, and, for hundreds of years, they spoke their own separate language.

It was not until the 1850s that Cornwall became, visibly, part of England. The Great Western Railway had reached as far as Plymouth, and the company wanted to push onwards into Cornwall. Their engineer decided to cross the Tamar at Saltash, at a point where the river narrows between two hills. Even so, the bridge is over a thousand feet wide. The water is strongly tidal, and is seventy feet deep at high tide. To make matters worse, the Admiralty demanded a headroom of a hundred feet so that warships based at Plymouth could pass underneath. The engineer's solution was bold, and indeed dramatic: one enormously high central pier with an iron structure, partly arch and partly suspension, on top. It is not a beautiful bridge, but, after more than a hundred years, it still looks original and still has an air of tremendous authority. On either end is blazoned the name: *I. K. Brunel Engineer.*

The genius of Brunel thrust the railway on into Cornwall. When he came to deep, wooded valleys, he soared across them, with viaducts built of pitch pine like the props of the Cornish mines. Cornwall, at last, was linked with the outer world.

Even so, change came very slowly. Cars were hardly seen on the Cornish roads until the 1920s, and, even then, not many. The first road bridge upstream over the Tamar was at Gunnislake, eighteen miles from the coast. It was only thirteen feet wide. Otherwise, cars had to join the queue, which grew more wearisome year by year, for the chain ferry from Plymouth to Torpoint. Not until the 1960s was a road bridge placed beside

Brunel's railway bridge. Now, hundreds of people drive over it every day from Cornwall to work in Plymouth. Some of their cars have a GB plate, but others have a plate saying 'Kernow' instead. This is the old Cornish name for Cornwall, and it serves as a last reminder that Cornwall was long something different, not really a part of England at all.

What was it like, this secret and separate life that the people of Cornwall lived for so long? As so often happens, the first thing we know about them is not of the way they lived, but the way they died. Four thousand years or more ago, the people who lived on this sea-battered, wind-tossed peninsula started to build massive tombs. They took huge slabs of the local granite and arranged them to form a room, tall enough, in one case, for a man to ride through on horseback. Then, on the top, they somehow levered a vast single slab of granite to act as the roof. In Cornwall these burial chambers are known as 'quoits'. Originally, they were covered by earth, but this has worn away and they now stand open to wind and rain. Some, like Lanyon Quoit and Trevethy Quoit, can be seen from a car window. Others, like Chun Quoit and Zennor Quoit, are in places no longer frequented. They can only be reached by narrow tracks through the gorse and the sharp-stemmed heather.

The people who built the quoits left other monuments. On the lonely downs near Liskeard are three adjoining circles of standing stones. They are known as 'the Hurlers' because one attempt to explain them was that they were young men who were turned to stone for playing games on a Sunday. Stranger still is the stone with a hole, known by its Cornish name of the Men-an-Tol. The stone is big enough for a man to crawl through, and, like the stone circles, was probably the scene of a religious ritual. Until recently, the local people believed that a child who was passed through the stone could be cured of rickets.

Gradually, these early Cornishmen, whoever they were, were joined by settlers from Europe. The newcomers may have been drawn by the mineral wealth which lies under Cornwall's stony soil. The story of Cornwall passes from mystery to something that can be, in part, understood. The men themselves are still there, curled up in their shallow graves at Harlyn Bay cemetery. So are their villages, like Chysauster and Carn Euny. Here we can see how Cornishmen lived at about the time of the birth of Christ. They lived in large huts of several rooms, grouped round a central courtyard. Chysauster, indeed, contains England's oldest semi-detached. They built underground rooms, maybe for storage, that bear the Cornish name of a 'fougou'. The whole layout is more elaborate than many visitors expect. To complete their surprise, there are water channels taken into the courtyards. Here, independent of the Romans, are the first houses in England with a supply of running water.

Archaeologists consider these Cornish remains to be very important, second only to those around Stonehenge. To the non-specialist, important ruins are often no more than a heap of old stones. Those in Cornwall are something more. It is astonishing how many people have confessed, almost unwillingly, that some Cornish sites have a very strong atmosphere. It is almost as if the stones have absorbed the feelings of men in the past, and now have a power of their own to generate feelings back. There is a strange sense in Cornwall of men listening and watching for something beyond the everyday world. The men who built the stone circles had a mysterious ritual to do with the sun and the planets. In 1901, Marconi, in a little hut near the Lizard, was the first man to transmit and receive radio signals across the Atlantic Ocean. Nowadays, the satellite tracking station on Goonhilly Downs has ultra-modern equipment for listening to noises from outer space.

The Cornish landscape itself helps to produce this feeling of strangeness. Few other counties in England can show such extremes. The rocky north coast of Cornwall, with long, slow rollers surging in from the Atlantic and with no land for thousands of miles, is a complete contrast from the moist, wooded creeks and enclosed harbours of the south. Different, too, is the granite spine of the county, where the trees may still grow stunted and bent, as if to show that nowhere in Cornwall is very far from the sea.

The first two areas are equally well known. Cornwall, along with Devon, is one of the main holiday regions of England, our national answer to the Costa Brava. As travellers battle their way along the narrow roads of the southwest, with full vocal accompaniment from the children in the back seat, they must sometimes wonder if it would be quicker to fly to Spain. A few Cornish cream teas later, they wonder if it would be cheaper as well. Here is a tragic dilemma. Cornish people, faced with a very short season, try to make enough money for the whole year. Holiday-makers resent the inflated prices. Next year, they may come back with a caravan in order to save the hotel bills. This makes the roads even more crowded, and brings less money into the district.

Is Cornwall, in fact, a substitute for Spain? For one thing, it is much wetter. Its reputation as a warm county is also rather misleading. It may escape frosts in the winter, but in summer the damp sea winds often keep the temperatures down below those in London. To go to Cornwall instead of going abroad can be to go home feeling cheated. The point is to go to Cornwall for what Cornwall alone can offer.

The north coast has the rocks and the sea, and the best surfing in England. To the holiday-maker, this means a lively tussle with surging Atlantic breakers, and, if he has any sense whatsoever, an eye on the red flags. Every year brings its tragic group of people who ignored warnings and saw one of their family drowned. But there are a few to whom surfing means more than this. To live with the waves and to understand them, this is a way of life. There are young men who come to Cornwall and take part-time jobs simply to live with the surf.

To the less energetic, the north coast is still exciting. The air is keen and lively, and on warm days which bring out the scent of heather and gorse, it can be intoxicating. Then, too, there is the quality of the light. This is such a tiny expanse of land in so vast a sea, and sometimes the barren rocks and the sweep of sand at low tide seem to give back light into the air. A hundred years ago, at the time when painters were starting to work out of doors rather than in their studios, this special quality of the Cornish light was recognized. Since then, Cornwall has been a centre for artists. Some, such as Ben Nicholson, Barbara Hepworth the sculptor, and Bernard Leach the potter, have given the little fishing port of St Ives an international reputation. Not all modern Cornish artists paint recognizable pictures of their surroundings, but much of their work derives from Cornwall, from the shape of stones and the patterns of light and water. One Cornish artist who did paint just what he saw was an old fisherman called Alfred Wallis. Wallis was quite untrained, and, because he was very poor, he often painted on scraps of cardboard. No one has captured better the colour of Cornish seas on a stormy day, when they are grey and yet rich at the same time.

The south coast of Cornwall is a different world. This is the English Channel, not the Atlantic. The waves have a less majestic swell, and the air is milder. This is the coast of fishing villages, clinging to the steep hillsides above their close, compact harbours. On a sunny day, when the sea is a deep greeny blue, and the roses flower under cottage walls in the tumbling, narrow streets, and fat seagulls preen themselves on the harbour walls, it can be enchanting.

Because it faces the Continent, this is the coast for smugglers, and sometimes whole communities, such as Polperro, were engaged in the trade. Smuggling is not a crime that most people take very seriously, because it is offending against 'the law' but not against individuals. The classic comment on law enforcement in Cornwall comes in *The Pirates of Penzance*, 'a policeman's lot is not a happy one'. So the smugglers have been romanticized, and they are thought of as cheerful, picturesque figures, who provide the theme for the décor in village pubs and souvenir shops. Yet, as so often in Cornwall, there is a darker side to the business.

With smuggling sometimes went wrecking, luring vessels on to the rocks by means of false lights. The Lizard peninsula, sticking out so sharply into the sea, was an ideal place for this. On nights when the moon was low, ships would be drawn on to the jagged rocks till they ran aground. The sailors who swam ashore might be killed as they lay exhausted in the foam on the beach, for 'dead men tell no tales'.

Wrecking bred its own terrors. For a long time, the Cornish believed that the souls of drowned sailors, denied Christian burial, had no rest. On a dark winter night, with no light in the street and little inside the house, it must have been easy to think that the cry of seagulls was really the cry of doomed men. Much Cornish superstition has this undercurrent of fear. It cannot be disguised entirely by the modern trade in plastic piskies and mermaids. These were the creatures of the Cornishman's two worlds: the moors where he might become lost amidst desolation, and the sea, which a man might hate, but was drawn back to again and again, until in the end, he drowned, and lay with the fishes and crabs.

Nowadays, Cornish wrecks provide a quarry for underwater archaeologists. The richest find so far has been the *Association*, Sir Cloudesley Shovell's flagship which was wrecked off the Scillies. The contents were sold at auction, and reached, among other things, what must be a world record price for a battered old pewter chamber pot. With the prospect of big money, a new breed of lawbreaker has appeared in Cornwall, the underwater pirate. These men do not report their own finds to the Receiver of Wrecks, and they hang about ready to plunder wrecks found by others.

One aspect of southern Cornwall that has no darker undertones is the gardens. They have Cornish-sounding names like Trelissick, Penjerrick, and Glendurgan, and are set in deep, narrow valleys leading down to the Fal and Helford Rivers. In winter the air is mild, and in summer it may become steamy. Here, exotic plants can be grown more easily than elsewhere in England, so that when new species are introduced, like rhododendrons in the last century, Cornwall is one of the first places where they are grown. These Cornish gardens are at their best in the spring and the early summer. The magnolias are star-like against the sky, and the camellias in sheltered corners are thick with bloom like a Chinese embroidery. The rhododendrons, spilling down to the water, are almost savage in colour; a sharp pink or the red of freshly-spilt blood. Later come the hydrangeas, that range in colour from vivid red to a piercing blue. In St Just-in-Roseland, set on a hillside above a creek, the churchyard is transformed into a garden. In summer, too, come the heavy, droopy flowers of herbaceous borders. On a warm day, the only sound is the hum of bees, and the only movement is of butterfly wings; a bright, exotic Red Admiral beside the delicate colours of a silver-washed fritillary.

Compared to the coasts, inland Cornwall is not very much visited. Towns like Launceston and Bodmin may suffer from through traffic, but not many people, bound for the beaches, stop there. It is on the coast that the great parking problem arises. Polperro has taken the step of forbidding cars to enter. Newquay, one wet afternoon, achieved the town planners' final nightmare: the traffic seized up so that cars could neither get in or out of the town.

Inland, once off the main roads, traffic is easier. Cornish lanes are narrow and high-banked, sometimes completely overshadowed by arching trees. A stranger to the district is likely to drive, very fast or very slowly according to temperament, with his eyes fixed rigidly straight ahead. When he meets another car, face to face in the narrowest part of the lane, he looks disbelieving, and the vehicles confront one another like two unwieldy prehistoric monsters preparing to do battle. In the end, one monster has to back. It is usually the local driver, who will have taken note of possible passing places as he went along. If, as too often happens, the stranger goes past without any nod of acknowledgement, he will have left a small trace of resentment behind.

To the patient and curious-minded, to those who are not surprised to find tractors and cows in a country lane, inland Cornwall is very well worth exploring. There is nothing spectacular there. The wildest and lushest of the scenery is to be found on the coasts. Nor are there any great buildings in Cornwall. It is too poor and too isolated, and it has had no great landowners to take an interest in its affairs. For over six hundred years, the title of Duke of Cornwall has gone to the King's eldest son, and few reigning dukes have bothered to visit their duchy. But many Cornish houses are very appealing, such as Trerice with its curly gables and peacocks sunning themselves by the old farm buildings, or Lanhydrock with its superb plaster ceiling, set in a green oasis near a desert of china clay mines. Sometimes a house has associations that stretch far beyond Cornwall. When Drake came home from the first English voyage round the world, he stored his treasure in Trematon Castle near Plymouth Sound. Part of the castle still stands, and a newer house within its walls is the home of Lord Caradon, who used to represent Britain at the United Nations.

Perhaps the most moving of all Cornish houses is Cotehele, hidden away on the high, wooded banks of the Tamar. It was built in early Tudor times, but Cornwall was always a little behind the fashion, and so, with its tapestry-hung rooms, its wooden beams and its cobblestones, it seems like the perfect setting for a medieval romance. On the first floor is a room called the solar, where the ladies of the house spent much of their time. A peephole is cut in one wall so that they could keep an eye on the servants in the great hall. But their main attention might be on a knight who had just ridden into the courtyard, a falcon on his gloved wrist.

Cornwall's village churches can offer this same sense of having stepped back in time. The county has been too poor to adopt every change in architectural fashion, and the Cornish have been a people who liked familiar things. Only four hundred years ago, which is not a very long time as history goes, they objected to having the Prayer Book put into English instead of Latin. They argued that if people could not understand either language it was better to keep to the one they were used to.

So it is that the village church of St Neot, a small village tucked well away off the road, turns out to have some of the finest medieval stained glass in England. All round the church, the windows tell stories. One is the Creation, and, whether or not by accident, the serpent tempting Eve looks like a medieval monk. Another tells of the Flood, and the animals going into the Ark have exactly that smug expression, well known to all pet owners, of an animal that is making its master work. A third tells in hideous detail of the torturing of St George. It is set behind the congregation, so as not to be visible during the service, which must have disappointed generations of small boys.

In Cornwall, too, an amazing amount of wood carving has survived from before the time of the Reformation. Launceston has a rare, early wooden pulpit, and in Altarnun church is a mass of wonderful carving, all done for the sum of £13 6s 8d (£13·33). That was back in the reign of Henry VIII. Altarnun, on the edge of Bodmin Moor, has a charm often lacking in Cornish inland villages, and is currently 'the best-kept village in Cornwall'. The name means 'the altar of Nonna', and St Nonna, who came from Wales in the sixth century, was the mother of St David. The church is not quite so old as that, but the babies of Altarnun can still be christened in a font that is over a thousand years old. On the four corners of the font are vast bearded faces, still with faint traces of colour. If the babies' brothers or sisters feel bored during the ceremony, they are of just the right height to examine the bench, that is pew, ends. On these are carved lively figures like a man with a cauldron, a fool, and a man playing the bagpipes. A child who escapes his parents entirely and wriggles up to the chancel may see, for what reason it is hard to imagine, a glass case with two stuffed owls.

Anyone who wonders about people in the past can study the

list of the vicars of Altarnun. Under Queen Elizabeth I, and again under Cromwell, the vicar was persecuted for refusing to change his religious opinions. In more settled times, another rose to become Archbishop of York. But perhaps the strangest memorial tablet in Cornwall is in Landulph church near the Tamar. Here is buried Theodore Paleologus, whose family had been the last rulers of Byzantium or Constantinople. Their court had been as magnificent and as formalized as anything that had ever been known in the world. Now, a few generations after the fall of Constantinople, one of their number had come to rest in this remote, obscure church. What strange path had brought him there?

Many men who have made the long journey to Cornwall have had an other-worldly character that fits well with the place. None have left more mark than the Celtic saints, whose names are on almost every signpost. More villages in Cornwall are called after a local saint than in any other part of the British Isles; such as St Cleer, St Ewe, and St Erney, St Erth, and St Clether, even St Veep, and St Teath. Who in fact were these people? Their names are almost unknown in other parts of England, and one dictionary of saints ignores them except for the remark that Cornish saints are 'a special case'.

There are plenty of local stories about them. Often, the saints are said to have come from over the sea by miraculous means. A young girl called Ia was standing on the coast in Ireland when she saw a leaf floating on the sea. As she gazed at it, it grew in size until she could step on it. She took this as a sign from God that she was meant to go on a journey. She drifted across to Cornwall, where she is now known as St Ives. St Pirran was seized by robbers in Ireland, who threw him into the sea tied on to a millstone. Instead of drowning, he floated safely to Cornwall, and landed on Penhale Sands. Once in Cornwall, the saints worked many miracles. St Tudy carried live coals in his tunic, and it was not burnt. He caused the tide to stop rising so that he was not drowned. St Petroc removed a splinter of wood from a dragon's eye. He cured a woman by making her vomit up a snake, three feet long, which had been making her ill since she swallowed it many years before.

What is the truth behind all these stories? They belong to the darkest of the Dark Ages, the gap between Roman and Saxon rule, when Cornwall was a separate kingdom. Because of its moors and its swamps and forests, Cornwall was almost cut off from England by land. It could be reached by water, however, and to the people of Ireland, South Wales and Brittany, Cornwall made an easy landfall. In all these places were Christian communities, that flourished independent of Rome and the Pope. It is not surprising that they should send holy men to Cornwall. Maybe some of them came in tiny frail craft, such as a little round coracle, which helped to give rise to the legends.

Once in Cornwall, the holy men seem to have stayed in one place. They lived very simply, praying and fasting. The local people would bring them a little food, and often leave fragments of their own clothing tied on to thorn trees nearby, as an offering to the holy place. To most modern eyes, the hermit would be an eccentric figure, sparsely clad, unwashed, living in conditions that became more and more filthy. In the early centuries of Christianity, his disregard for all cares of the body turned him into a saint. This is what the word 'saint' means in Cornwall, simply a man who was looked on as such by the local people.

The idea that some places were holy ground lingered for centuries after the saints had gone. As recently as one hundred years ago, the Cornish are said to have fastened rags to the trees near a holy well. Until recently, it was believed that the waters of Dupath Well could cure children of whooping cough. It is not surprising. Dupath Well is one of those places where centuries of worship have left their own impact. To hear the flow of the spring water, to feel it, icy-cold even on a hot day, is to wonder for how many centuries before Christ some unknown god of the spring had been worshipped there.

In more recent times, two great creative geniuses of religion have visited Cornwall. One was George Fox, the first Quaker, a man who refused to accept the established forms of religion, or the very unequal social structure of his own day. He paid for his protests by being imprisoned in Doomsdale in Launceston Castle, a 'nasty, stinking place' which had not been cleaned out for many years. They could not even sit down, for the filth came right above the tops of their shoes. A happier link with Fox is that the oldest Quaker meeting house in the country is in Cornwall, at a place called Come-to-Good.

That was in the seventeenth century. A hundred years later, one of the greatest figures in all Cornish history took Cornwall by storm. He was John Wesley, the founder of Methodism. At the time of his coming, the people of Cornwall were very poor. They were apathetic about religion, which meant little more than a bishop in far-away Exeter who very seldom bothered to come and see them. They were intensely superstitious. When Wesley came to them, preaching the love of God and repentance for sin, they jeered and attacked him at first, but later came in their hundreds, then in their thousands, to hear him. This passionate, but yet realistic man, tells in his *Journals* of how he made more than thirty journeys to Cornwall: riding around in the wind and the driving rain; often afflicted with toothache; and preaching to multitudes in the open air, at places like the old mine workings at Gwennap. Cornwall was never the same again. When great hardship came to the people in the next century, the faith that Wesley had given them helped them to bear it. But his was no passive faith. He also inspired the wish to improve an often unjust social system, and it is no coincidence that the Cornish Farmers' Union is one of the oldest unions in the country.

The spirit of Wesley also helped to revive the Church of England in Cornwall. At last, Cornwall had its own cathedral at Truro, the first English cathedral, apart from the rebuilding of St Paul's, to be built since the Middle Ages. For the first time in a thousand years, Cornwall had its own bishop again. One of his earliest actions was to ride out to Gwennap in teeming rain to pay his own tribute to 'glorious old John'. But the Cornish church did not follow the plain and simple style of the Methodists. That would be to underestimate the Cornish love of extremes. Instead, it followed a new trend for more ornamentation in churches and more Catholic forms of service. The small village church at Blisland was redecorated at this time, and there are few churches in England that give a stronger sense of having stepped right back into the Middle Ages. From nineteenth-century Cornwall, too, comes one of the most popular of all modern church services. It was Stephen Hawker of Morwenstow, well known as a poet as well as a clergyman, who introduced Harvest Festival.

Cornwall's connection with those who reject the society of their own times has not yet come to an end. Nowadays it attracts the drop-outs, the hippies or whatever the current term may be. They are not solitary, like their forerunners, but flock in large numbers to places like Newquay and St Ives. The townspeople, who live on the goodwill of other tourists, resent them. A beard and flowing garments are no longer taken in Cornwall as a sign of being a saint. They attack the incomers' standards of hygiene in the same spirit, if more genteel terms, as George Fox attacked those of his jailers. The hippies, in turn, feel that they are being picked on simply because they are different. 'They say we look odd,' a long-haired girl argued on television. She pointed at crowds of shoppers in plastic macintoshes. 'Doesn't it occur to them that they look odd as well? At least, I'm not going round wrapped up in a polythene bag.' Only time will show if the drop-outs include any genuine visionaries, who will add something new to Cornwall's long history of spiritual exploration.

The mystical associations of Cornwall come out in romantic literature, for which Cornwall has long been a setting. Most famous of all are the legends about King Arthur. Arthur, as a person in history, seems to have been a sixth-century war-leader, not really a king at all, who fought the invading Saxons. As time went on, more and more stories, often very moving and picturesque ones, became attached to his name. In the end, he came to be thought of as a chivalrous hero who ruled over a picturesque medieval court. Some of the legends about him were linked to places in Cornwall.

The chief of these is Tintagel, where, according to later tradition, Arthur himself was born. Anyone who explores Tintagel Castle may start to doubt this, as the place was built several hundred years after the time when Arthur is supposed to have lived. The early remains are not of a castle but of a monastery. In fact, there is no real evidence to connect Arthur with Tintagel. Nonetheless, the idea that the great British hero was born there has a sort of poetic truth. The situation of the place is superb. It is set on sheer rocks, jutting out into a sea that is sometimes raging and boiling, sometimes placid and jewel-like in colour. The air is exhilarating, especially on a wild day when it is necessary to cling to the rocks for shelter against the spray and the wind. The modern village, on the headland above, is guaranteed to bring anyone down to earth in the shortest possible time.

Tintagel also comes into the story of Tristran and Iseult. This is one of the world's classic stories, of lovers who were enthralled by a magic potion and doomed to death by their love. Once again, the magnificent setting matches the intensity of the subject. Once again, too, there is no proof that they ever went to Tintagel. What has been found is a connection between Iseult's husband, Mark, King of Cornwall, and a hill fort near Fowey known as Castle Dore. In the same way, some truth has been claimed for the legend, also linked with the Arthurian stories, of the lost land of Lyonesse. Once there may have been land between Land's End and the Scillies which is now covered by sea. As so often happens with legends, time has become telescoped and confused.

No truth has been found for the story that connects King Arthur with Dozmary Pool on Bodmin Moor. This flat, dark expanse of water with bleak moorland around it is claimed as the place where Sir Bedivere threw Arthur's sword after his death, and where a mysterious arm rose up out of the water to seize it. Visitors now may find that the most mysterious thing about Dozmary is a notice from the farmer nearby asking them not to walk on the hedge. This sounds an uncomfortable, if not an impossible undertaking, but in fact the word 'hedge' in Cornwall means a bank of earth and stones.

In modern times, Cornwall has been a favourite setting for stories of adventure and romance. The most famous is Daphne du Maurier's *Rebecca*, which contains a very vivid description of a great house and its gardens beside the sea. Here is Cornwall at its lushest and most flamboyant, and the book has coloured many people's idea of the county. This is a little ironical, since Daphne du Maurier has also written of Cornwall in many other different moods. Another very popular kind of book is that which expresses people's dream of retiring to Cornwall, away from the noise and stresses of city life. Derek Tangye's descriptions of life as a flower grower, and the birds and animals which have shared his experiences, put into words what many readers would like to do if only they had the courage to give up their jobs. Or would they really like it? Another writer who sought a new way of life in Cornwall is Denys Val Baker. His experiences, described in *Adventures Before Fifty*, have been, to say the least, mixed. Anybody who dreams of 'getting away from it all' in Cornwall ought first to read his description of how the sea came into the kitchen.

Perhaps those who know best the particular quality of life in Cornwall are the children who grow up there. Unlike many modern children, they are still seeing the world that their parents and grandparents knew. Not for them the tower blocks and urban motorways of a concrete city, but instead a world still largely governed by the change of the seasons, where the children of a village school recently gave up their spare time to help safeguard the local badgers. A child's world in Cornwall was beautifully evoked by Anne Treneer in *School House in the Wind*. Though she wrote of the past, her flowering headland above the sea has not changed in essentials. A writer who speaks for modern Cornish children is Charles Causley, in haunting and deceptively simple verse. In one poem he describes children performing their own ritual round a tomb in order to

> 'hear a dead man
> Speaking underground.'

Like so much in Cornwall, this combines fantasy with a harsh, often brutal reality.

The harshness of much Cornish life is brought out by the ever-present signs of Cornish mines. For thousands of years, Cornishmen have lived by digging wealth out of the earth. In a book written at the time of Julius Caesar, and based on still earlier sources, an island off the British coast is described. At high tide, it was completely cut off from the mainland, but at low tide it could be reached by a causeway. The local inhabitants used to load their wagons with tin, and take them across at low tide to trade with foreign ships. The description fits St Michael's Mount, near Penzance.

The visible signs of mining in Cornwall are much more recent than this. In the eighteenth century came the Industrial Revolution and the invention of steam-powered engines to do work which previously had been done by men or animals. For a short time, Cornwall the backward, Cornwall the remote, was in the very forefront of industrial progress. There was a wealth of metals: tin, copper, and lead; and also of traditional mining skills. The famous engineers, Boulton and Watt, supplied engines to be used in the Cornish mines for raising loads to the surface. They sent a Scotsman called William Murdock to supervise the work of installing them. While he was in Cornwall, he made an important invention of his own. He lit his house by coal gas, which provided the brightest light that had yet been known. It may have seemed the complete answer to lighting, but only a few years later, a Cornishman called Humphry Davy opened up new fields for scientific research by his work on electricity. He also invented the miner's safety lamp. Until then, many miners had been killed by explosions of the gas called fire damp, which were set off by a naked flame, so the invention has saved large numbers of lives.

The Cornish mining industry flourished. Just over a hundred years ago, the now quiet and somnolent Tamar Valley was loud with the clank of machinery and the thump and throb of paddle steamers coming upstream to collect the ore. The villages were crowded with people who worked long hours down the mines. The traditional Cornish pasty is a useful pre-packed meal for taking underground, and one story says it ought to be made so solid that it can be thrown down a mine-shaft without breaking.

But time was against Cornwall. The copper-bearing lodes wore out, and big new deposits were found overseas. Then there was the question of fuel. Unlike other growing industrial areas, the west country had no coal to power the engine houses and pumping machinery. In the Tamar Valley, engines were worked, according to a long tradition, by water-powered wheels. This seemed very old-fashioned in the nineteenth century, which was the age of coal, although it is coal which now seems out of date today.

So Cornwall became, most tragically, a county of ghost mines, and thousands of Cornish miners had to emigrate overseas. They took their skills with them, and in mining districts in the United States the traditional Cornish names starting Tre-, Pol-, and Pen- can often be found. They left behind desolation, which the damp air of Cornwall has now softened with growing things. A book on *The Industrial Archaeology of the Tamar Valley* by Frank Booker has aroused a new interest in Cornish mining, and an industrial museum has been established at Morwhellham on the Devon bank of the Tamar. Old quays have been cleared, and old machinery has been rescued. But in nearby Calstock and Gunnislake, once busy communities on the Cornish bank of the Tamar, the level of unemployment is among the highest in Britain.

Anybody who is interested in old machinery can see a number of beam engines preserved at Pool near Camborne, but the most striking remains of Cornwall's industrial past are the old engine houses. These are usually built of the local granite; tall, austere, and narrow, with a chimney stack beside them. Some are set near the sea, so that the mine workings stretch out under the water. The sight of a roofless engine house on a rocky headland, where nothing grows except heather and gorse, with the sea foaming far beneath it, and the sun setting in the west, so that both water and land are ablaze with colour is unbelievably dramatic, even by the dramatic standards of Cornwall.

Although the traditional metals are now no longer mined, Cornwall still lives very largely by what are given the ugly name of the 'extractive industries', in other words digging stuff up. Slate quarrying is an old tradition, as is shown by the many finely-carved slate tombs in Cornish churches. Nowadays, the Delabole Slate Quarry near Tintagel is the largest in England. The chief industry of the county, though, is mining for china clay. This started two hundred years ago when a Plymouth chemist called Cookworthy made the first English porcelain. The clay is also now used as a glaze for paper, and in medicines for upset stomachs. The industry has completely transformed the landscape. Enormous mountains of clay waste tower over inland Cornwall, visible from forty miles off in Devon. When the sun catches on them, they gleam with an unearthly, faintly metallic glow. The obvious comparison is to a lunar landscape, and, in fact, they have been used for filming a television series about another planet. The tips grow and grow, for to every ton of fine clay there are eight tons of waste. No softening grass can take root on their barren slopes, for it would soon be smothered by still more clay. Nor has anyone yet found the answer for the tons of waste that pour out into the sea near Par, staining the water a whitish grey for hundreds of yards offshore.

One of the strangest places in Cornwall is called Roche Rocks. On top of a sheer pinnacle of rock is perched an old hermit's chapel where, so legend says, a leper once lived. The chapel can now be reached by climbing two steep iron ladders. From the top, can be seen the most extraordinary landscape. First comes the primeval Cornwall of bracken and jagged outcrops of rock. Next are some recent additions: sheds made of that building material so popular in Cornwall, corrugated iron; a rather stark modern housing estate; and a starker graveyard. Beyond that, the landscape seems to have suffered some giant convulsion, that has thrown up clay heaps and chimney stacks on a more than human scale. There is nothing whatsoever beautiful in the scene, though it could make a powerful painting, but here, more than in almost any other single place, is the very essence of Cornwall. On the one hand is mysticism, in the old hermit's chapel; on the other is mining, on which Cornwall's life depends.

Cornwall's future is tied up with the clay pits to an almost frightening extent. What jobs will there be for Cornish children when they leave school? The tourist trade provides summer work only. Fishing is in decline. Once Cornish fishermen caught pilchards for food, now some of them have to take summer visitors fishing for shark for amusement. Falmouth, the biggest port in Cornwall, has a very large number of men out of work. There have been suggestions that it can be made a container port, but then it would be handicapped by the bad communications between Cornwall and the rest of England. Attempts have been made to revive tin mining but nothing serious has yet been achieved. The prospect of taking oil from the 'Celtic Sea' is still in the future. For the moment, the county wants to attract light industry, perhaps from overseas firms, but again the very bad road system is a disadvantage. There are even rumours from time to time that the railway link between Plymouth and Penzance may be closed down. Once more, Cornwall would be almost cut off from the rest of England.

In this situation, the china clay industry has been Cornwall's main hope. The recent news that it was going to pay off eight hundred men was a shattering blow. It is small comfort to a county that it should attract the elderly and retired, and those escaping the 'rat race', if it cannot provide enough jobs to stop its own young people leaving.

This problem faces the whole southwestern peninsula, Devon and Cornwall alike. To the outsider, the obvious thing is that they should stand together. Unfortunately, both sides still cling to their old suspicions that a different breed of men lives on the other side of the Tamar. In some circles, it is still a matter for grave family doubts when a young man from Plymouth marries a girl from Saltash. At present, Plymouth, the biggest city in Devon, is split from Cornwall on a number of local issues; such as widening the Tamar road bridge, and building a power station on the Cornish side of Plymouth Sound. Soon, there may be some friction about making new reservoirs, for the wet southwest is perpetually short of water. The region could do with an airport, but the question of where to put one is guaranteed to provoke many a quarrel.

The Cornish have gone so far as to start their own nationalist movement, the *Mebyon Kernow*, or Sons of Cornwall. Politically speaking, it cannot be said to have achieved much, but it has helped arouse an awareness of Cornish traditions. The ancient Cornish language is once again being studied. It is made known to a wider public by the paper table napkins that *Mebyon Kernow* sell, so that if anyone happens to know that 'tre' means a village, 'pol' a pool, and 'golowjy' a lighthouse, this is probably how they found out. There has also been a revival of interest in Cornish literature, and recently translations of traditional plays were performed in the open air theatre of Pirran Round.

Assuming that the economic problems are sorted out, can Cornwall keep its own character? This is a problem shared by all holiday regions. The coastline becomes a long string of featureless hotels and holiday flats that are empty for much of the year, as has been happening along the shores of the Mediterranean. The villages are 'done up' and their charm can become synthetic. In the end, the tourists, with their flood of cars and caravans, destroy the beauty and peace that they came to look for.

Cornwall has two advantages over the Mediterranean coast. One is the National Trust, which has already preserved open spaces on many fine headlands. The other is the fierce and battering sea. This stops the actual face of the cliffs being used as a building site, in the way that is being done in some parts of the Mediterranean. Clearly, there must be new building. Holiday-makers want something to do on a wet afternoon, and, what is too often forgotten, the young people who stay in Cornwall want something to do on a winter evening. The best hope is that the centres of interest should become concentrated and provide more entertainment, while long stretches of coast remain undisturbed.

Inland Cornwall is less likely to change, for it does not have so much obvious beauty to draw the crowds. In places, the very ground may be dangerous, for among the short, windswept grass and the gorse bushes are the shafts of long disused mines with strange names like the Ding Dong. Here, in deserted places, slabs of granite stand upright, as they were planted four thousand years ago, and there is a bleakness and a mystery that modern life has not touched.

LITTLE KINGDOM

by Richard Church

Kent is one of the most surprising counties in England. So many people think of it as a long, straggling suburb of London, with its northern shores along the Thames Estuary one dreary stretch of factories and docks. Other folk, especially foreigners and our own people who come and go between Great Britain and the Continent, see it merely as a corridor between London and the two seaports, Dover and Folkestone. Though now that most journeys from our island to the mainland are by air, the corridor theory is diminishing.

In fact, Kent is a most varied and beautiful 'little kingdom', as I called it in a book of that title, which I compiled some years ago. In that book I let writers and all kinds of men and women speak for themselves, through the two thousand years in which Kent has been a concise corner, the extreme southeastern projection of the island of Great Britain. Julius Caesar spoke first, describing his landing there, and his defeat in the year 55 B.C. He was the first person to be surprised by Kent. He had expected an easy landing, to capture Britain as a means of out-flanking the Germanic hordes of northern Europe, who were always a menace to the Roman Empire. He wrote: 'But the enemy knew their ground; they could hurl their weapons boldly from dry land or shallow water, and gallop their horses which were trained in this kind of work. Our men were terrified. They lacked that dash and drive which always characterized their land battles.'

But Caesar came to terms with the Britons, exchanged hostages, and noted that the Celtic people were not savages. They had been in contact with Rome, Carthage and Phoenicia for centuries, trading their tin. They even had a gold coinage, which is always a sign of a well-established culture.

Of course, Caesar came back the following year, with an army and navy powerful enough for the job which the far-seeing Caesar had in mind. That was the beginning of Kent's known history. The story of the county before that coming of the Romans is a job for the archaeologists; but one fact is certain: Kent was the part of Great Britain which first became an organized, one might say civilized, community. The reason for that is obvious. Kent really *was* the corridor through which traffic with the rest of the known world at that time was carried on. The tin mined in Cornwall, and the white china clay, came up along the Tin Road (part of which is often confused with the Pilgrims' Way which stretches from Winchester to Canterbury), and was shipped on the galleys which carried this precious raw material to the great cities of the Mediterranean, a trade that went on long before the Christian era. And trading means contacts, with people and with ideas. It means exchange of goods, and the sophistications of society and the arts.

So Kent was already a flourishing civilization when the Romans came and conquered, to bring even greater wealth of ideas, in building, engineering, and way of life in general. They planted vineyards, and built magnificent villas, some of them palaces, particularly along the northern slope of the Downs running along the Thames Estuary. Richborough near Deal was the military headquarters, and the huge enclosure of the camp there survives today. From Richborough the Roman rule and culture spread through the country as far as the Welsh borders and the wall which the Emperor Hadrian built on the Scottish border.

The Germanic tribes continued through the four hundred years of the Roman occupation to harass the coasts of Kent. Here was a ripe fruit for the picking! But the Romans kept them out by organizing a fleet and soldiers under a general commissioned for that particular purpose. Thus the county thrived, until the Empire was struck at its heart, Rome, by more direct attacks from the Nordic folk, many of them rebellious troops in the Roman legions.

In A.D. 411 the legions in Britain were withdrawn to help defend Rome, and that left Kent, as well as East Anglia and Yorkshire, at the mercy of the sea-wolves from Jutland, Norway and other lands where the Nordic folk were becoming better organized and increasingly powerful, so much so that they were to split the Roman Empire into two. But that is another and much longer story, which I cannot discuss here, except to say that the history of Kent has always been deeply involved in it. I am not sure that the story is finished even now, in the latter part of the twentieth century. Future generations, born in Kent, will have to deal with that.

The historian J. R. Green, who published a *History of England* in 1874 which is still enchanting to read, wrote: 'It is with the landing of Hengist and his war-band at Ebbsfleet on the shores of the Isle of Thanet that English history begins'. But in the hundred years since he said that, we have learned much about what is called pre-history, and this puts back the horizon of history more and more into the distant past. As I have said, Kent had many centuries of civil growth even before the Romans came. Just up the hill going out of Maidstone on the road to Chatham, stands a heap of gigantic stones called Kits Coty House. Other stones lie farther down the fields, set in positions which puzzle the archaeologists, just as similar formations in Stonehenge have done. Who put them there? Where were they brought from, at great expense of thought and labour? And for what reason?

The answers are many, but they all point to the fact that immigrants into Britain came, wave after wave, over great periods of time, bringing with them from the Near East their own culture and their own worship, probably that of the sun, a very obvious object for veneration. We call that worship Mithraism, adopted and elaborated by the great Persian civilization three thousand years ago. It probably controlled the way of life in Kent for centuries, in what were then the strange, lonely forests and downlands. Kent was at that time mostly forest, one great stretch called Anderida which stood in what is now the Weald, from Folkestone for 140 miles into Hampshire.

Bit by bit, that forest was eaten into by mankind, for fuel, for building houses and ships, for baking into charcoal to smelt the iron ore which abounds in the soil of the Weald. The rusty trickles of water in the little streams that drain into the Kentish rivers still show that trace of iron in the soil.

So, with the advance of civilization and the growth of the population, the Forest of Anderida has almost disappeared. The Saxons, a farming folk, first made clearings in the forest, which they called 'denes', where they introduced their pigs who fed on the acorns of the native oak, the predominant tree. Many of our Kentish villages have names ending in 'den', and we know what that implies, in village history.

I have written about the surprises which Kent can spring on people who are ignorant of its history and have not explored its amazing variety of scene and natural character. Caesar's was the first surprise from the historical point of view, and I will mention two others of the same kind, before I go closer to the soil to try to explain why Kent is so full of minor surprises for the person exploring there for the first time, and indeed for the hundredth time.

The first Teutonic invasion was made by the Saxons, who penetrated to west Kent, beyond the shores of the River Medway, which rises over the boundary near Edenbridge in Surrey, and roughly divides the county of Kent into two. Those folk, now of course diluted with many mixtures of blood, we still call Kentish Men. A later wave of invaders, from Jutland, dark-haired folk called Jutes, settled in Thanet and east of the Medway. Their descendants today are called Men of Kent. It is all rather theoretical now, for time and historical circumstances have stirred the mixture without pause, but there are still little bits of solid sense floating about in the amusing distinction.

The second surprise was for the Frankish Norman, William the Conqueror, who in 1066 invaded from Normandy and vanquished and killed the Kentish King of England, Harold Godwin, who had succeeded Edward the Confessor, a saintly Christian, but ineffectual ruler. To call him that reveals that I have said nothing about the coming to England of the new faith, in the sixth century, when Ethelbert, King of Southern England with his headquarters in Kent, married Bertha, daughter of the King of Paris. She was a Christian, and brought her priests with her. So when in the year A.D. 597 Pope Gregory sent the missionary Augustine to convert what the poor saint believed to be barbarians, the job was already half-done. Ethelbert was persuaded into the Christian faith, which was at that time still fervent and pure. He gave Augustine a site in Canterbury and another in Rochester, to build churches and establish brotherhoods. That was the most positive establishment of Christianity in Britain, though this gentle faith had still to contend with the incoming Danes, who worshipped the gods of Valhalla, the deities of the northern pine-forests and the grim solitudes of the long northern winters.

Both the English and the Normans were supposedly Christian when the dynastic clash came in 1066, and that may have been the cause of the comparatively humane conquest by William. I say comparatively, because we should have thought it horrifying today, though all conquests imply terrible suffering for poor innocent folk who are probably unaware of what is going on until they see their homes going up in flames and their families being slaughtered. Warfare never changes its spots, and the spots are spots of blood.

William proposed to rule England by the social organization called the feudal system, which obtained in Normandy. By this, the king, who represented the state, was owner of the land. He leased it out to his nobles, whose eldest sons inherited, and were responsible for raising troops when needed for protection of the throne (which was the state). It was really a rational and sensible organization of any community, for it kept the estates together, turned out the younger sons to further enterprise, and made the holder of the estate responsible for his people. But it was a servile state, involving a kind of bondage to the community which is being revived in our time in many parts of the world, both politically and economically.

But the people of Kent stood out against William of Normandy, and would accept him as King of England only on their own terms. He agreed. The feudal system was not introduced into Kent and the county kept its Saxon rule of *gavelkind*, by which a landowner's estate after his death was divided between his sons. That led to the growth of a body of small gentry in Kent, large in number but each with few acres. Only gradually did powerful barons intrude there. Even six hundred years later, when civil war broke out between King Charles I and Parliament, these deep-rooted gentry of Kent, though divided among themselves during the war, survived the chaos, and were able to resist the bureaucracy imposed by Parliament during Cromwell's Protectorate, and the corruption of Court intrigue after the restoration of the monarchy in 1660.

It was out of this unique independence that several further surprises struck the governments of successive kings when religious tyranny, or unfair taxation, weighed too heavily upon the country. The revolts always came out of Kent. The most violent of these was that led by Wat Tyler, an ex-soldier from Chatham, in 1381, when young Richard II was king. Earlier in that century, during the reign of his grandfather Edward III, a terrible outbreak of plague, called the Black Death, had swept across Europe. It wiped out more than half the population of England. The value and power of the working people rose accordingly. Crowds from East Anglia crossed into Kent, and joined the folk who had united under Wat Tyler. This rabble army was strong enough to reach London, and murder the two people who represented the unbearable tyranny of the great barons and the Church, Archbishop Sudbury and Lord Saye and Sele. The young King Richard made well-meaning promises of reform when he met the insurgents on Tower Hill in London, but one of his followers, the Mayor of London, stabbed Wat Tyler and killed him. The revolt collapsed. So did another one seventy years later, led by another Kentish man, Jack Cade, who met with the same fate.

Such has been the story of the people of Kent. Their general character has been fashioned by their geographical setting as a frontier county, the stepping-off ground to the mainland of Europe, and the stepping-on ground from it. This has meant a constant coming and going of travellers of all kinds, connected with international politics and business, and all the humane contacts and wealth of relationships in cultural, religious, artistic and domestic affairs, in which Kent has always been so intimately involved.

Thus we find in the people of Kent these two characteristics, due to the interaction of their geographical and historical position. On the one hand is the deep-rootedness of a large number of small landowners, many of them purely Saxon in origin, along with even more lowly folk not unlike the peasantry of France, whose families have never known the serfdom of the feudal system. On the other hand, there is this constant quick-change of settlers, coming and going, from the Low Countries, from France, and from London, passers-by in law, commerce, politics and other social activities, who have been drawn, during the intercourse of two thousand years, by the attraction, what I would call the *genius* of the county. Some of them have been successful statesmen, who have founded families in Kent, and by their abilities acquired large estates. I think of the Sackvilles, the Stanhopes, the Sidneys, whose noble homes survive today; distinctions in stone, or rose-red brick, to add grandeur to the generally modest rural scene, of farmhouse and cottage, the smaller signatures of a long-established democracy.

Mainly from the small gentry, and those great families, have risen from time to time individuals of genius, whose names survive in world history, because of what they did in their lifetime as soldiers, statesmen, scientists and artists. I have written elsewhere about the county, 'Turn a stone and you start a poet'. It is true. The way of life in Kent, and the variety and intimate appeal of its natural features, have an inspiring effect upon people living within their influence. Kent is a rich county in every way; rich in its population, and the continuity of that population's activities. Through the Middle Ages and into the eighteenth century, Kent with Sussex produced the iron used for all purposes. It produced the cannon that armed the oaken ships of war which helped to defeat the Spanish Armada in 1588. The railings which Christopher Wren put round his mighty St Paul's Cathedral, were foundried and smithied in the village of Lamberhurst in the extreme western border of Kent. For centuries the iron industry was a principal source of the county's wealth. So too was the woollen trade, and later the silk trade brought by refugee Huguenots from France, driven out because of their Protestant faith.

The Flemish weavers, invited to England by the shrewd King Edward III, brought their wealth and their craftsmanship to Kent, where they settled first in Cranbrook, beginning by rebuilding the church there so magnificently that to this day it is called the Cathedral of the Weald.

Those Flemish weavers also brought another source of ultimate wealth to Kent. It was the hopbine, with which they proposed to flavour the English small-beer more to their liking. Seventy per cent of the hops used in brewing British beer today are grown in Kent. It is a form of farming that demands much initial capital, but the profits are large. Two of the world's greatest brewers have estates in Kent consisting of hop gardens. The fields where the hops are grown are called 'gardens' because of some legal squabble centuries ago, in which the vicar of Goudhurst was involved, connected with land taxes.

Thus as one activity has waned, another has waxed, and Kent has never been without an industry to bring riches into the county. North Kent, on the Thames Estuary side of the North Downs, is now largely industrialized, with much variety of trades, outstanding among them that of paper-making, which includes everything in that form from coarse packaging to newsprint and fine-art papers used in water-colour painting. The famous Whatman paper beloved by artists has been made in Maidstone by a family firm named Balston, in their mansion called Springfield, for generation after generation. The house is now the nucleus of the many buildings of the Kent Education Committee and the County Library, both bodies to be praised for their encouragement of cultural life in the county. The large brewing combine of Whitbread-Fremlin are also helpful in this good work. They establish literary competitions for school children, and offer guided tours round the hop gardens near Paddock Wood during the weeks in late summer when the hops are being gathered, dried and stored in large sacks called 'pockets' for later use in the breweries.

In the midst of the extensive block of brewery buildings in Maidstone, the county town, there stands a Tudor building, an old grammar school. The town council had proposed to pull it down, but the brewers bought it, and have converted it into a staff canteen and club, without defacing it. Such acts of sensitive preservation are welcome today, for the growth of population and consequent traffic in Kent are a constant threat to the relics of its past history and its natural beauty. A similar fine job was done recently by the firm of millers who owned the windmill at Cranbrook. A team of Dutch craftsmen was brought over to restore the mill, which was built in 1814 by a man named Dobell, whose cousin Sydney Dobell was a poet of some fame in the Victorian Age.

These good works are examples of the way in which Kent unites its people, gentry, tradesmen, and farmers into a true democracy, with mutual interests. There is a rhyme made by the immortal poet *Anonymous* in the fourteenth century, which probably reveals the secret of this intelligent and harmonious fusion in the social structure of Kentish folk. Prosperity can make for kindliness as well as for self-satisfaction. Here is the rhyme:

A Knight of Cales,
A Nobleman of Wales,
And a laird of the North Countree;
A Yeoman of Kent
With his yearly rent
Will buy them out all three.

When that was written, Kent was probably the richest county in England, its only rivals being the three counties of East Anglia, north of the Thames Estuary, but also with seaboard facing the Continent, offering close commerce and cultural contact with the Low Countries and France.

It was from Kent that a native of Tenterden went out to Bruges as representatives of the Guild of Merchant Adventurers, a medieval organization mostly of merchants in the wool trade, at that time the principal source of our national wealth. That is why to this day the Lord Chancellor sits in the House of Lords on a Woolsack, which is the symbol still of our national prosperity, with the inference that law and order, scholarship and the arts, are dependent upon well-ordered and successful industry and commerce. Some critics and philosophers are inclined to say of this theory that 'it is not necessarily so', and they could bring much evidence to prove their point.

Nevertheless, Kent's prosperity over so many centuries must account for the many great people born and brought up in the county. The one who went to Bruges and represented the English Merchant Adventurers for a quarter of a century was William Caxton. As well as being a successful businessman, he was also a scholar, who translated many of the classical texts which he read in manuscript. He met another with similar interests, one Gutenberg, born in the German town of Mainz, but working for some years in Strasburg. His work was the replacing of handwriting by moulded type, handmade of course, but capable of being used again and again. That was the birth of printing, a step forward in civil communication comparable to the introduction of radio and television to the world of today. That is a long story, which is still not ended. Caxton learned the craft from Gutenberg, or possibly from a pupil named Colard Mansion in Bruges. He came back to England, an elderly man aflame with enthusiasm and energy, and King Edward IV, shrewd and imaginative, patronized the project of setting up a printing press in London. Space was given to Caxton in the Almonry of Westminster Palace, and there this great son of Kent set up the cultural revolution whose processes are thundering down Fleet Street and all over the world today. One of the first of his productions was the known poetry in English, especially his beloved Chaucer's *Canterbury Tales*.

I have been dealing with Kent's people first, so I may as well mention a few more, preparatory to saying something about the land itself, and the influence its contours, its position in this oddly-shaped island, its soil and landscapes, has had upon its inhabitants.

Another great practical philosopher, which is the right classification in which to place Caxton, was a man born in Folkestone, into a family prosperous in commerce since the reign of Henry III. William Harvey was baptized, according to the Canterbury Cathedral Register, on 6 April 1578. He was one of a large family, whose parents were well-off and owned several farms in the district. He spent much of his childhood in the country and showed a precocious interest in nature and its workings. This led him to biological research, and to medicine. He never left this interest, and he went to the right college in Cambridge to advance his studies, Gonville and Caius. Thence he went to Padua, in Italy, at that time the most famous university in Europe for the study of medicine. He spent two years there, and came home with the degree of Doctor of Medicine. He made a wise marriage within the profession, to the daughter of the Queen's physician. Later he became Physician to King Charles I, leading Physician to the ancient hospital of St Bartholomew, and an influential Fellow of the newly-created Royal College of Physicians. He had many disciples, for his researches made him famous throughout Europe. He also had some enemies, for he did not suffer fools and pedants gladly, and was given to explosions of hot temper when he was thwarted or his discoveries queried. His greatest discovery was that of the circulation of the blood. That sounds simple enough, but nobody, not even Aristotle or Galen, the classical founders of the science, as distinct from the *art* of medicine, had discovered that simple fact. It was as simple as Galileo's discovery that the earth was round.

He was not satisfied with that achievement. He explored still further, and published a book about the generative processes of all animal life, probing into what is still the mystery of the composition of the blood. His work as a natural philosopher, which has put him in a class with Newton, was carried on while he led a full life as a famous practitioner, and an administrator who differentiated the fields of work, as between the physician, the surgeon and the pharmacist. He died in 1657. A statue of him stands on the Leas, in Folkestone, in a lovely setting, for the sea-front of Folkestone, with the wooded slope of the Leas dropping down to the sea, is surely the most handsome in northern Europe. Its dignity befits the character of this great man.

Another example of outstanding genius, as distinguished from great talent, is the work of a young man born in Canterbury in 1564, the year in which his fellow poet and dramatist, Shakespeare was born. But he was not level-headed like Shakespeare, who lived to be elderly and made a comfortable fortune, which enabled him to retire to his birthplace. That did not happen to the shoemaker's son, Christopher Marlowe, of Canterbury. His father was a prosperous craftsman and an alderman. His mother was the daughter of a Protestant priest who had been defrocked during the reign of Mary I, when the Catholic rule was temporarily restored as the state faith. Through his mother, Marlowe may have begun to take the road of scholarship. He was probably the first of all scholarship boys, for he went to the King's School in Canterbury on a scholarship founded by Archbishop Cranmer.

Another scholarship took him to Corpus Christi College, Cambridge. He took his degree in 1584. This was done in spite of mysterious absences from College. Some recent discoveries of documents in the Patent Office by an American researcher reveal that he went abroad on these occasions, and the theory is that his brilliant scholarship and general ability had brought him to the notice of Sir Francis Walsingham, who worked for Queen Elizabeth and the shrewd statesman Robert Cecil. Walsingham built up a Secret Service in which the young poet was employed.

He was never punished for his absences from College. But the punishment came later, and from his masters. He was a proud character, scornful of people of high birth who were inferior to him intellectually. He therefore got false ideas of his own importance, and talked too much. This is believed, today, to account for the incident that took place in a lodging in Greenwich, within the royal precincts where no quarrelling or duelling was allowed. In what appeared to be a drunken brawl, Marlowe was stabbed in the brain with his own dagger. But the brawl was staged, for the other men involved were also secret agents employed by Walsingham. Marlowe's indiscreet tongue was his downfall, as well as his glory.

He was a poet whose genius was the forerunner to that of Shakespeare. His fiery and impetuous blank verse introduced a new medium into drama, which Shakespeare took up and fulfilled.

Marlowe was not the only literary pioneer of Kentish birth. Philip Sidney produced what may be called the first novel in the English language, and Thomas Wyat introduced the sonnet, that fourteen line poetic form invented by an Italian monk three hundred years earlier, later to be used by poets in every language of the Western World.

Both these immortals were men of action as well as writers, as indeed were most writers of the sixteenth century, before the writing of books had become a professional occupation. Philip Sidney was an aristocrat, nephew of Queen Elizabeth's favourite, Robert Dudley, the Earl of Leicester. His father was a courtier and diplomat, whose country seat was Penshurst Place, near Tonbridge, where Philip was born in 1554. Nothing he wrote was published in his lifetime, but he was a prolific writer of poetry which is still read, and author of that first novel in our language, called *Arcadia*, which is read only by students of literary history.

His life story is too well known for me to repeat it here, except to quote what a French critic has said: 'He was not only the perfect knight, but also the lettered courtier'. His character was noble, and he was beloved by the Queen, the Court, and the people of England. Fighting against the Spaniards in Flanders, he was mortally wounded at the Battle of Zutphen in 1586, where he made the gesture which sums up his character and his exemplary life. 'Your need is greater than mine,' he murmured to a wounded soldier lying near him on the field of battle, as he handed him the mug of water which both so desperately needed.

Thomas Wyat was born at Allington Castle, near Maidstone, in 1483, the son of an official at the Court of Henry VIII. He too became a diplomat, after taking his degree at Cambridge. He served in France and Italy, which accounts for his knowledge of the two languages and their literatures. As well as the sonnet he introduced other Italian verse forms into English poetry, and he used them with a vigour and power which lost none of the native speech rhythm.

I must also mention a poet born in 1536, who spent his later life at Knole, the great mansion outside Sevenoaks. He was Thomas Sackville, first Earl of Dorset, great son of a great father. Both held posts equivalent to that of Prime Minister. Thomas married the daughter of Sir John Baker, of Sissinghurst Castle, near Cranbrook. Baker was Chancellor to King Henry VIII, as Sackville became to Queen Elizabeth.

Sackville was a statesman of such integrity and ability that the Queen rewarded him with the gift of Knole. He, like Philip Sidney, was a gifted poet who added greatly to the rich literary output of that Golden Age, which lasted through the Queen's reign and well into the seventeenth century. Sackville wrote somewhat in the manner of Chaucer, with sagacity and worldly wisdom tempered by nobility of character.

People who know Kent intimately will not be surprised that writers and artists have been born, or migrated there, without interruption ever since that Golden Age. The Sackville family, in a recent daughter of that ancient line, produced Victoria Sackville-West, born at Knole in 1892. Her poetry and novels have made her famous in the twentieth century. Her long poem *The Land* is perhaps the most passionate and detailed evocation of the genius of the county. It portrays the folk, the scenery, the very soil of the Weald.

So does the early poetry of Edmund Blunden, who was the

son of the schoolmaster in the village of Yalding. And another writer who died in 1959, Frank Kendon, also captures in his verse and prose the spirit of the Weald. He was born near Goudhurst, in 1893, a year later than Victoria Sackville-West at Knole, twenty miles away. I could mention many others of our time. Faithful sons and daughters of Kent are still being born, some of whom will also be spokesmen of the county, its singular qualities, and its defects.

For there are defects also, the worst of them Kent's tendency to become over-populated as the industrial drift south-eastward is maintained. But we cannot be certain about the future, and some sociologists say that already there are signs that, under wise governmental guidance, this overloading in the south is being slowed down. Even so, the general growth of population means the addition of characterless suburbs to most of our Kentish villages and towns, necessary and comfortable, but adding nothing to the distinctive features of the rural and urban architecture of the county. But Kent is not alone in this elimination of local characteristics, which the evolution of the Industrial Age has so suddenly accelerated throughout Europe. If the Channel Tunnel is made, the multiple consequences will speed up those changes in Kentish life even more violently. So I had better turn from the description of Kentish people to say something about the county itself; its geography, and what I would call its *mystery*, using that word in the old-fashioned meaning, as of trying to get into its very nature, its beauty, and the factors which have, in their entirety, given Kent the reputation of being 'the garden of England'.

The outstanding feature of Kent is the wide variety of scenery within so small an area, for the county is only some 80 miles long from London to Dover, and 40 miles wide from north to south at its western frontier. But it has a bit of everything, except snowclad mountains. It has a long coastline; the Thames Estuary on the north, where once the Roman civil servants had their villas; the North Sea round the Isle of Thanet to eastward; and the English Channel to the south, where that gem of English seaside towns, Folkestone, is situated on a promontory where the North Downs turn abruptly southward by the Elham Valley, to end at Shakespeare Cliff and the Warren, between Folkestone and Dover. Both towns are ports, and Dover is really Britain's front door, or it used to be until the age of the aeroplane. Folkestone and Dover, each so full of character, are only 21 miles from the Continent, and this geographical factor has played a great part in their history. The Romans had a fortress and lighthouse on the top of Dover Cliff, and later William of Normandy built the castle there which still stands frowning across the Channel. To balance this threat, Folkestone's lovely Leas, graceful and dignified, offer a welcome to visitors from abroad.

Immediately west of Folkestone, the hill drops to a wide stretch of marshland which did not exist a few hundred years ago. The higher ground inland was formerly the coastline and is now sloping farmland blessed with magnificent views across the marsh and out to sea. That Romney Marsh, named after one of the villages on a ridge bordering it, where formerly the sea reached, has silted up before the conflict of currents where the tides coming down the North Sea are mis-timed by nature with those coming up the Channel. But Nature, with human assistance, has also worked quickly to cover the marshland with soil, and we see it today as a vast fertile grazing ground for the famous Romney Marsh sheep. Dykes, instead of hedges, divide the landscape there, and a river called the Rother runs southward through it; a capricious stream that has the habit of occasionally changing its course.

The few people of the Marsh have been a community unto themselves, of a secretive habit. Now a great atomic power station has been built on the shingle of Dungeness, a nose of the Marsh sticking out to sea. That will inevitably change the nature of the folk there, by adding some hundreds of technical experts to the fisherfolk and graziers who have been the sole inhabitants since it first began to silt up in the late Middle Ages. In those days, the sea came up to Smallhithe, near Tenterden, where boat-building was the principal occupation. Now Smallhithe consists of a few old cottages, in one of which the famous actress Ellen Terry had her country home. The National Trust keeps it as she left it, and visitors can go there to see the relics of her life and fame.

The cause of the great variety of scenery in Kent is its less recent geological changes. The county was once part of an almost Alpine range running east to west. That range has decayed like a great tooth, the heights subsiding and leaving northern and southern edges, the Downs, with the Weald between them. Thus all manner of subsoils have come to the surface, each stratum with its own mineral content, with iron dominant through the Weald, and lime in the form of chalk over the Downs. Various kinds of clay and gravel also come to the surface where the different strata turn upward like the edges of a saucer; a very chipped saucer.

Each of these soils has its own predominant vegetation. Once the great Forest of Anderida, mainly of oak and birch, ran from Folkestone westward through the county. I have explained why that forest has disappeared under the iron-founding and agriculture of mankind. But the iron in the soil of the Weald survives to enrich the layer upon layer of rich humus which always gathers in woodlands. That is why the Weald has become prime land for growing fruit and hops, as well as cereal crops.

That rich soil also accounts for the many small towns and villages which have grown there. I say 'grown', because most of them are so much part of the soil that one cannot imagine them having been *built*. I have called them, in my history of Kent, 'rose-red villages', and so they are, with their medieval tiling and those small tudor bricks, decorated with weather-boarding, which is another marked feature of the architecture of the county. The human settlements are innumerable, amid hundreds of isolated farmhouses and manors. This has led to the making of a maze of narrow roads and lanes, which cover the county like a net over a woman's hair. Never was a countryside so confusing to the tourist, especially as so many of the signposts contradict each other, or appear to do so if the stranger does not realize that in Kent there are at least six ways of approaching every village.

How different are the Downs! The North Downs are mostly wooded, with great beech trees which love chalky soil. The South Downs are bare, under a quilting of turf, like velvet, though since two world wars demanded enlargement of farmlands, they have had to be cultivated. But there are still wide stretches of open country that run westward into Sussex. The poets Hilaire Belloc and Rudyard Kipling have said, or rather sung, much about that particular glory. In another book I have become prosily lyrical myself, with these words: 'When I think of chalk I think also of southwest winds blowing against those slopes and whistling in the grasses and flowerets dwarfed by centuries of sheep-cropping'. There is no other countryside quite like the South Downs. They are an intoxication.

I wish I could describe a mere dozen of the many villages which punctuate the county with their individual characters. Right through the Weald, from Westerham, where General Wolfe was born, to Bishopsbourne near Deal, where the great novelist Joseph Conrad lived, they lie self-contained, with their ancient churches, their big houses and their cottages where once the wool-weaving was done. Some were rich in those medieval days. Cranbrook is shown on the large map of England in the Uffizi Palace, in Florence, where the great bankers, the Medici family, kept their accounts. They had money invested in the wool trade of Kent. Goudhurst, on its hilltop, is another such village. So are Tenterden, Biddenden and many more, all still to be seen only slightly spoiled by modernity and the motor car.

At the heart of the county stands Canterbury, with its cathedral whose spiritual foundation was laid in the year

A.D. 597, when St Augustine came and converted King Ethelbert. After Thomas à Becket was murdered in the cathedral (on the spot which can be seen there today) in 1170, his shrine became one of the most frequented places of pilgrimage in Europe, until in 1539 it was removed by the Protestant government. For those three hundred and fifty years Canterbury profited by catering for the pilgrims. It was soon to recover from the loss, when the French Huguenots settled in the town as silk weavers.

The cathedral is among the most beautiful Gothic buildings in northern Europe. It still attracts visitors from all parts of the world. They bring much to Canterbury, and take much from it, for as I have written in my book on Kent in the *County Series*, 'Poetry, music, all the arts, together with a sense of history, and the dominance of religious vision in all its manifestations of power – these are the forces demanded from the mind and soul of the pilgrim to Canterbury, belated though he may be.' But we can say the same of Rochester Cathedral, which was the second Christian monument to be built in England; and indeed every village church in the county of Kent survives as a reminder of what civilization means, in terms of faith, that mental and spiritual vitality in mankind which for nearly two thousand years has worked upon the natural character of Kent, adding to its forests, downs and plains the signs of our handiwork as an ever-growing community.

Perhaps the most methodical way to look at this combination of natural formation and mankind's developments upon it, is to assume that Kent is fan-shaped, with London as the hinge from which it can be spread out. Looking towards it, southeast, as from Sydenham Hill, the explorer will have the left-hand feather of the fan as the River Thames shore running along the north of the county, with the Isle of Sheppey about halfway to the extreme tip of the North Foreland. The land behind this shore soon rises to the North Downs, which might be called the second feather of the fan. They drop southward, over magnificent panoramas, the vast width of the Weald which again is divided by a lower ridge of hills halfway to the South Downs and the long stretches of Romney Marsh.

Each of these arms or feathers of the fan has its particular kind of soil and scenery. That Thames-side stretch, as far as Chatham, has become almost completely industrialized, as I have described. But it has its interesting places, such as Rochester and Gravesend, though the latter old town has lost its picturesque ferry across the estuary to Tilbury in Essex, this motorists' delight being replaced by the more practicable Dartford Tunnel. Faversham and Whitstable (famous for its oyster-beds) still keep relics of their historical character, and are worth a visit when driving eastward to the more open and rural reaches of the estuary where Herne Bay and Birchington look out over the widening waters of the Thames Estuary almost to the open sea.

Finally, by keeping to the coast, the explorer comes to Thanet, once an island cut off from the mainland by the two arms of the River Stour. But nature did some silting up there, as it did on the south coast of the county. Thanet is sea-girt, and enjoys sea weather, rough, clean, invigorating. That is why several resorts have sprung up round its coast; Margate, Broadstairs and Ramsgate, all popular holiday places, standing round the curve of the North Foreland, on the way south to Deal, Dover and the English Channel, with Folkestone pinned like a brooch at the point where the headland drops to Hythe, Sandwich and Romney Marsh.

But catalogues of places, like maps, can only point the way, as reminders and guides. They cannot convey the magic, the beauty, the character which the countryside, the towns and villages, the isolated farmsteads and the manor houses in their parks, possess in such abundance in Kent. The way down the right-hand feather of that fan which I have imagined offers one surprise after another as we explore down the county border adjoining first Surrey and then Sussex. The way is so near London, yet woodlands survive, farms stand amid their tillage and meadows, sudden vistas open out, giving southward upon glorious landscapes. But words fail me, and I am not sure that I am too anxious to betray the secret beauty-spots which I have known and loved all my life, being drawn more and more inevitably until I left London, my birthplace, and came to live in the very heart of Kent, not far over the border from Sussex, in an oasthouse near the enchanting village of Goudhurst. So now I have declared my secret. But a love for Kent is not a light which can be hidden under a bushel.

THE ROLLING, WINDY ACRES AND THE POWERFUL, TIMELESS SEA

by Pauline Clarke

East Anglia, that huge bulge which sweeps round from the spade-shaped tongue of the Wash in the north, to the wide, wriggling inlets of the Orwell, Stour, Colne and Blackwater rivers in the south, is a low-lying country, though not all so deadly level as the Fens, those black acres which lie south of the Wash into Cambridgeshire. Cutting off the Fens from the bulge there is a tract of downland connecting East Anglia with the Chilterns, which runs up to the coast at Brancaster and provides some delightful miniature hills and headlands in north Norfolk, as does the Cromer ridge. Because in ancient times the centre of the bulge was dark with forest, and the Fens were often under the sea, the trackways of early men ran along this higher, open ridge. Peddars Way starts on the Norfolk coast near Holme, and you can still walk along stretches of this grassy prehistoric track used by foot travellers into Suffolk. South of Thetford, the Icknield Way runs right down to the Thames at Goring. Roman, and modern, roads have both used and obliterated it. But beyond the ridge Norfolk and Suffolk tilt in a plateau down to the sea, their lazy rivers in gently sloping valleys.

Now these eastern lowlands have their compensations: one is an overwhelming sense of the vastness of the visible sky, bleak, or piled with a hurly-burly of clouds, or uninterruptedly blue, or splendidly fiery with sunsets and sunrises. Moreover, cold northerly winds bring that diamond-bright light, beloved by painters, which illuminates the world with a startling clarity. There is too the characteristic marsh and duneland of much of this coast: saltings purple with sea-lavender and green with samphire, whose mud cracks into chocolate-brown jigsaw pieces at seasons of low tide or drought; channels spiky with spartina, between emerald swathes of weed-covered, sandy mud where the cockles breathe; sand-dunes grey-green with waving marram grass where you can lie and scorch, though the world outside is swept with a brisk wind; sand-bars where seals bask in September suns; pebble beaches where yellow sea-poppy, blue sea-holly, and scented campion blow in June and July; but also, wide stretches of golden sand.

East Anglia's coastline, which has had so much to do with our history, was formed long ago – and is still being modified – by the sea eating away at its soft cliffs, and the currents and waves washing this stuff across the river mouths. The rivers, languid in so level a country, are thus deflected by great shingle spits. Blakeney Point and Scolt Head Island are built up of pebbles shifted west by the dominant waves. Below Caister, the beach material is carried southwards. In late Saxon times, the fishing settlement which was to become our gaudy Yarmouth was formed, but the River Yare was forced ever southwards by the drifting shingle, until groynes were built in Elizabethan times. At Orford Ness, the River Alde has to run twelve miles south to reach the sea. At Harwich harbour and Stour mouth a jetty across the spit has checked drifting material. (There would be none of those loaded container lorries from the Midlands, lined up at Parkestone Quay for Europe, if it were not so.)

What happens to the stretches of coast where the sea is filching cliff away, two to three yards a year? Places disappear: under the sea lies much of Dunwich, an important port in the time of Henry II, a monastic town, with many churches. It used to be said you could still sometimes hear their bells as the sea tumbled them.

In January 1953, a spring tide and onshore winds caused many east coast banks to break and the most disastrous flood since 1898 swept over the marsh like a tidal wave. Houses were destroyed, people and animals drowned, boats washed miles inshore. But we were able to see, from the medieval bridge at Wiveton two miles inland, what the ancient wide sweep of the River Glaven's channel must have been like before it silted up with the centuries: for the sea had, temporarily, taken it all back again.

This coastline, with its wide river mouths, sheltered inlets and easy landing-places, was a lure to invading peoples from Scandinavia and north Europe, looking for immediate plunder or for land to settle, and blown here in their various craft by the brisk easterly winds of early summer. Belgic Celts, Angles and Saxons, Vikings (or Northmen) all came in this way: the ports of King's Lynn, Yarmouth, Lowestoft, Southwold, Felixstowe, Harwich, Colchester and Maldon must have seen them come.

Inland lie the rolling, windy acres of Norfolk farmland, its charming hillocks surmounted with trees and bushes, coverts for pheasant and partridge (it is a great shooting country); the stretches of gravelly heathland aflame with gorse, broom and heather; the rich wheat lands of Suffolk and its pretty river valleys; and the great East Anglian towns, Norwich, Ipswich, Bury St Edmunds, Thetford. East Anglia is windy and sandy, low and dry, harsh, keen and bright, without much mystery: while the farther west you go the more undulating, green and lush the land becomes until you reach the romantic mountains of Wales. Are East Anglians prosaic, unmusical, and quirkily, matter-of-factly humorous, while the west breeds poetry, song, fire and fantasy? Perhaps. But the generalization is often untrue.

What goes on in East Anglia? To begin at the coast, fishing. From the great ports like Yarmouth and Lowestoft, and from innumerable humbler inlets, men have always fished, bringing in cod and haddock, hake and mackerel and the multitudinous herring. At Lowestoft fish harbour you need a permit for the quay, where in autumn Scottish girls come south to slit the herring for kippers, with flashing knives. So it is easier to get to know fishermen in smaller places (if it is ever easy to get to know fishermen: the Norfolk ones are often dour, proud, idiosyncratic, with that quality of apartness which has to do with the struggle against the sea). At Sheringham they will take you out to catch leaping, blue-green mottled mackerel. (Every hour out of the water makes a difference to the taste of a mackerel!) Cromer has always been famous for crabs; as has King's Lynn, with shrimps, prawns, cockles and mussels too (breeding seals in the Wash frighten off ordinary fish). At Wells they seem to specialize in whelks, and their harvest festival is a harvest of the sea. At Blakeney there are still a few mussel lays passed down jealously from father to son. On dark, icy mornings on an ebbing tide the fishermen will row down to the uncovering beds, take up a boatload with a curious hooked net called a whim, and come back on the rising tide. Once sorted with blue, numb fingers, they are now riddled with hand machines, to sieve the big from the small. A seasonal luxury, mussels are not enough to make a good living. No wonder that the younger men have taken to the lucrative trade of lug-worm digging. Boxes of worms go for bait to the fishing ports, and if you dig hard at low tide in the muddy sand, you can make a lot of money in a week. The paddling amateur, meanwhile, may collect samphire (poor man's asparagus: boil, dip in melted butter, and pull it off its delicate skeleton in the mouth). The Essex coast, particularly east of Colchester, is famous for oysters; at Mersea Island you can buy them on that part of the harbour revealingly called 'the old city'.

But not all sailors are fishermen: and there has always been trade up and down the east coast and across to the Continent. In the days of sail or 'salt-caked smoke-stack', conditions were tough for the young sailor. An old man told me hair-raising tales about the ship's cook when he was galley-boy. Once, driven to desperation, he left the ship at Sunderland determined to find another; and on her way home she was wrecked. Before this century the backbone of the trade of all these east coast ports (apart from fish and innumerable commodities of lesser value) was coal and grain. They took in coal from Newcastle and its neighbours and sent out grain brought by horse-drawn wagons from their farmlands. At Blakeney, whose harbour was dredged for trading vessels up to 1914, the last of the granaries has been made into a row of elegant houses. With the coming of the railway five miles inland to take the grain, and the development of bigger ports, Blakeney's harbour was abandoned to the silt, and its craft are now only small boats. The same kind of history can be traced at Woodbridge and Aldeburgh.

At Burnham Thorpe, where his father Edmund Nelson was rector, was born in 1758 England's greatest sailor, called Horatio after Horatio Walpole (the brother of the famous prime minister, Sir Robert, who was his mother's great-uncle). Nelson's upbringing was Spartan. His mother died when he was nine, and his father took on vigorously the role of both parents to his large family. Yet his childhood was obviously happy: when he was off Ushant in the *Victory* a year before his early death, he wrote with loving nostalgia: 'Most probably

I shall never see dear, dear Burnham again . . .' The country around the Burnhams (there are seven) and the two Creakes is still quiet, wooded and hilly; you can imagine the young Nelson enjoying his bird-nesting, tree-climbing, tiddler-catching. He must have smelt the sea often and heard perpetually the gentle summer thud or winter crash of the waves, when he and his brothers explored the marshes. He knew those winter Norfolk days when it is not fit to be out, and on one such he and his brother set off on ponies through the snow to get to school, Horatio being determined to go on, as their father had put them 'on their honour'. In 1768 they went as boarders to North Walsham. The grammar school here had been founded by Sir William Paston, whose family had hoarded their ancient letters at Oxnead, the family seat, to the lasting benefit of all later students of medieval Norfolk. Horatio knew Norwich, for he had been first at the Royal Grammar School, next to the Cathedral. He knew the little market town of Aylsham engaged in the Norfolk worsted industry. At Lynn he must have dashed down those narrow 'lokes' between the warehouses, to the quays, to see what ships were in or setting sail. One day in the Christmas holidays of 1770 he saw in a newspaper that his naval uncle, Captain Maurice Suckling (their great hero) was appointed captain of the *Raisonnable*, sixty-four guns. He begged to go with his uncle to sea. So at his own instigation, at twelve-and-a-half years old, Nelson's career, nourished in his heart on the Norfolk coast, began.

There is wild-fowling along the coast. In cold winter dawns before the sunrise stains the creeks crimson, the thigh-booted wild-fowler splashes off with his gun, or drops quietly down in his flat gun-punt overnight, to await the mallard, teal, and widgeon. One skipper we knew had had an accident years before in his punt and in true Nelson tradition lost half his right arm. Thereafter Will learned to do most things in a boat with his good arm, his teeth and his stump, and help was not welcomed. He would row strongly with both oars in one hand.

All along this coast too come smaller birds, some to breed

on sites now carefully guarded by the National Trust's bird-watchers at Scolt Head, Blakeney Point, Cley Marsh. Herons, tufted ducks, and shelduck haunt the marsh; you can see reed buntings and meadow pipits, and hear exaltations of skylarks above you. Waders of every kind leave spiky, fragile prints on the mud; white, fork-tailed, red-legged terns wheel; ringed plovers, oyster catchers and gulls call; or a bittern may 'boom' at Cley; and one famous year a sea-eagle was viewed from afar by many boatloads (he stayed in residence a suspiciously long time). The nesting sites of tern and oyster catcher are roped off now, and you can no longer walk carefully along the high shingle, find the greenish, blotched eggs, points together, almost hidden among the stones and shells, and stake the spot for the birdwatcher. When the young 'eggs-on-legs' are hatched, some terns, in particular the rare, nervously brave arctic, will dive-bomb the unwary visitor with wild screams of rage.

'Only small boats,' I said: but despite their lightness and frivolity (compared with traders and trawlers who work for a living), small boats can have sleekness, speed and enchantment. (Compare a racehorse with that solid fellow the Suffolk Punch, most famous working horse in the world.) At Brancaster, Overy Staithe, Morston, Blakeney, Aldeburgh, Woodbridge, Ipswich, Brightlingsea, Mersea, Maldon, congregate eager sailors on hot (or perishing) summer days. To see the boats lined up in the distance, their quivering sails looking almost ethereal, straining to be off on a race, is an uplifting sight. Almost as if they might be remembering how every seaworthy small boat from our southerly coasts made its best speed to Dunkerque beaches, in 1940, to take off the stranded British army. (Will's son went, and arriving back one evening somewhat the worse for wear, gave – and got – only a casual nod and wave from the fishermen on the 'carnser', as they call the quay.)

The Broads invite the sailor too. These great stretches of open water lie near the mouths of the Bure, Yare, and

Waveney Rivers. It used to be thought they were natural features, due to land subsidence and the silting that followed the piling of sediment across the rivers' mouths. Investigation suggests they are probably deep peat-diggings, flooded after they ceased to be dug at the end of the last century, and their shores made gradually shallower by mud and vegetation. Cruising quietly up some rushy stretch of grey-green river from your night's berth, past old mills, bridges, and abbey ruins, and then scudding across the wind-flecked broad, is a domestic kind of sailing best done in the less crowded off-seasons. Crowds can always be encountered at the big resorts, with their amusements and piers and fairs and lights: Felixstowe, Yarmouth, Cromer. ('The best of all the sea-bathing places,' said Mr Woodhouse about Cromer in Jane Austen's *Emma*, reflecting the growing popularity of sea visits and bathing at this time.)

Two other alluring subjects belong to the shore:-flotsam and smuggling. Flotsam – the stuff washed up – has always caused heart-searchings. In 1487 the Pastons are discussing, in one of those family letters, *whose* property is a great whale washed up 'against Thornham in the King's stream': Sir John Paston's, the King's, My Lord Admiral's, or the people of the country's? (Thornham now, significantly, is not on any stream and some way from the sea.) My experience extends to a coaling vessel which ran aground after jettisoning (in vain) most of her cargo. The 'people of the country' took things into their own hands, and the coal into their boats. Many quiet journeys were made and by the time some salvage policy was decided on, there was not much coal left.

As for smuggling, it is perennial. Parson Woodforde of Weston Longeville, a great Norfolk character whose diary covered many years of the eighteenth century (and who read the Paston Letters, newly discovered, to his niece Nancy) was often feverishly engaged in bottling, or perhaps burying, liquor, before the excise men came. He had tubs of brandy and Geneva (Dutch Gin) from 'Moonshine Buck', the blacksmith. Of such as he, Kipling wrote: 'Brandy for the parson . . .'. The customs men at Cley once met a wagon-load of barrels on the marsh (the smugglers vanished into the mist), impounded it in a customs shed and went off through a back door. Next morning, the shed was empty. The smugglers had sent a boy up to remove some tiles, drop down and unbolt the main doors. Some people think that the Shuck legends belonging to this coast and the Fens, were put about by 'the Gentlemen' to keep prying folk inside at nights. Shuck is a great, black, ghost dog with gleaming eyes and panting mouth. In Suffolk he seems to be sinister: but in northeast Norfolk he is the dog belonging to two drowned sailors, one washed up near Salthouse, the other near Brancaster: the faithful Shuck pads between the two. A friend (not a native but a 'furriner' as Norfolk calls them) once told me quite seriously that he had bumped into Shuck in his car.

East Anglia has always been rather proud of its way of talking (or perhaps it is the 'furriners' who notice and foster it). Dialect goes on, in spite of the BBC and the school teachers. The most individual points perhaps are the use of 'do' and 'don't', really meaning 'if I do', 'if you don't'. Someone telephones the doctor: 'He can't come to you, do he'd never get there. Come you today, don't he'll die'. Then there is the use of 'that' for 'it': 'tha's a fair way'; and the expressive double (or treble!) negative: 'Don't none of you never come back no more!' Norfolk people are undaunted by difficulty: the rabbit disease, myxomatosis, was simply called 'the old mixy-moxy'. There are many survivals too of old words and old pronunciations: 'coach' pronounced 'cooch' is 'to coax'; a dove is called a 'dow', pronounced 'doo'. And everybody 'goos' rather than 'goes'. I always think, listening at a distance, that it sounds Chaucerian, and maybe many of those old sounds have lingered on.

Inland, East Anglia has always been primarily agricultural. Grain grows by the mile: what the poet Traherne calls 'orient and immortal wheat' ripens in billowing golden acres, solid and uninterrupted by the thistles or red poppies of years ago; silvery oats, bearded barley much used previously for malting, wheat, the last to turn. It is also a great place for roots, particularly since the revolution in agriculture which was taking place slowly, locally, but certainly, from the late sixteenth century onwards. In medieval times, when the grass failed in winter, men slaughtered and salted most of their food animals. The sixteenth century saw farmers trying to overcome this problem: alternating grass with other crops; draining fen and marsh (with the help of Dutch engineers) for more pasture; flooding fields to get lush April grass for ewes and lambs, and more hay; experimenting with manures other than animal ones; growing fodder crops like clover; most important of all, growing roots for winter animal feed. Carrots were grown in the sandlings along the Suffolk coast from 1597 and soon spread to Norfolk. The turnip first took a hold in that part they still call High Suffolk (not that it is high – but the grass and wheat grow high) from about 1650, and thereafter in east Norfolk and the heathlands. By the 1670s Sir Robert Walpole (who was to build himself a splendid turreted stone hall at Houghton – a secretive place, but you can just see it through its parklands) was growing it up there. And before 1700, so was Lord Townshend at Raynham Hall nearby: he is always called Turnip Townshend because it was said, inaccurately, that he had introduced the seed first. Last of the great Norfolk landholders to grow the turnip was the Earl of Leicester, 'Coke of Norfolk', who had William Kent, the great architect of the Palladian manner, build Holkham Hall, and who managed to wrest some reward from his bare and sandy acres. (You can visit Holkham, as people did when it was built: but of the four great Norfolk houses, the loveliest is the Jacobean Blickling whose warm, rosy fabric and mysterious yew hedges are so much more desirable than Holkham's yellow brick or Houghton's stone grandeur.)

After this period, wintering animals on turnip, swedes and cabbages became general, better stock could be bred, dairying and the supply of fresh meat could go on in winter. Since the improved order in which crops were grown, and different fields were used, was pursued most uniformly in east Norfolk, it came to be called the Norfolk system, or more loosely, the Norfolk rotation. The basis of modern farming methods was laid. So East Anglia is important in the history of farming. If you go to an agricultural show now you will see the cream of this region's animals: milk and beef cattle (including the new 'Charlies' – Charolais from France), sheep, goats, sleek oiled pigs, Suffolk Punches, Percherons, and shire horses, and every kind of poultry.

The fields are varied and beautiful: a stretch of blue cabbages or neat rows of purplish sage for the packeting firms; or the sudden shrill yellow of mustard (prepared almost exclusively by Colman's of Norwich). And acres of the polished green leaves of sugar beet, supplementing imported cane sugar. Nowadays the beet are 'topped' by machinery: but I have watched men following the tractor as it turned up the rows. Armed with a sharp knife, they prodded the beet, slashed off the leaves and tossed the root into the tumbril with a rhythmical precision beautiful to see.

Fruit grows too, both orchard and soft fruit; the rich Fen soil is superb for soft fruit and market gardens. This has led to jam, canning and freezing industries. When that frightening thing, a fen blow, occurs, a high wind picks up the light black soil and carries it in clouds, darkening the day and lifting the farmers' sugar beet, onion, or carrots out of the ground.

And what about sheep? Where are the vast flocks of sheep that grazed East Anglia between the thirteenth and eighteenth centuries? There *are* sheep still, but they have not the sovereign importance they had then when they supplied wool, a major export to Europe, and manured land which would not otherwise have borne even the barley crop. They grazed the heathlands and Brecklands of Norfolk, coming along grassy drove-ways or 'drifts' from the townships and going back to be folded at night on the tilled fields, to manure them. In summer they were fatted on northern salt marsh, or Fen pastures which many reached by the old drove road still traceable from Hockwold Fen across Breckland. In Suffolk the heaths of the coastal sandlings were the main sheep walks, with the salt marshes for fattening: and all round the Thames and Essex estuaries sheep fed on the saltings (Sheppey, after all, means Sheep Island).

Great wealth followed, in medieval times, the export of raw wool, and East Anglia, because of its easy access to the Continent, and its good communications inland, was in an excellent position. There had always been spinning and weaving for home use, and as the cloth industry developed in East Anglia, often with the help of Flemish weavers, so prosperity grew. Colchester and Coggeshall (where you can still see the timbered house of the rich wool-merchant, Thomas Paycocke), Sudbury and Kersey (the most enchanting small village in Suffolk, and which gave its name to the cloth 'kerseymere'), Clare and Cavendish, Long Melford and Lavenham became busy centres of the cloth industry. And in Norfolk, first Worstead (after which is called any cloth of fine, combed fibres which has not been 'felted' or matted) and then Norwich, rose to predominance. Guilds, in some ways like trade unions today, grew up. In Norwich the spinners and dyers, the combers and fullers, the weavers and the worsted weavers (notice all those surnames!) had their guilds. (Woollen cloth, unlike worsted, is felted, by being cleaned and thickened with fuller's earth, or 'fulled'. Norwich specialized mainly in worsteds.) The trade guilds acted different parts in the medieval mystery plays, which traced the creation, fall, and salvation of mankind, and were usually performed at Corpus Christi time. All over East Anglia you can see splendid fifteenth-century churches, flint guildhalls or richly-beamed ones as at Lavenham, lavishly built and decorated with the wealth from wool.

The cloth trade flourished until the eighteenth century, much spinning and weaving being done at home. In 1783 Parson Woodforde recounts a visit to Norwich to see 'Bishop

Blaize's Procession'. (St Blaize was the patron saint of the wool-combers, for tradition said his flesh was torn by hooks: the combers 'teased' the threads of wool with teasels, grown for the purpose.) Then, first in Essex, later in Suffolk, and in Norfolk and Norwich last, the industry dwindled and declined. The main reason was the growth of the mechanized textile industries, woollen and cotton, in Yorkshire and Lancashire. Manufacturers invented machines both for weaving and spinning: in factories they produced the goods more cheaply. East Anglians, proud of their craft, often rejected machines. The north had soft water for cheaper fulling and dyeing, while East Anglia's was mainly hard. It had coal to power the machines and East Anglia had none. Perhaps its people (low be it spoken) had less conservative natures.

The Brecklands, those ancient sheep-walks of Norfolk, are, like the Broads, unique in England. They are wild open heaths, with a very thin layer of sandy, gravelly soil over the underlying chalk which covers much of East Anglia. They extend in a rough rectangle between Thetford, Elveden, Brandon, Watton and East Harling, and their poor soil would only produce a crop (after intensive sheep manuring) once, say, in seven years. So it was divided into 'brecks' (breaks) which were broken up in turn, and then allowed to go back to heathland. Nowadays, though there are still some cultivated fields, the Forestry Commission makes plantations of tidy conifers which are harvested like any other crop. Admittedly they are not our natural mixed forest, but their scent is aromatic and in most places you can walk through them – even sight some timid young fawns in the trees, as we have done. Between the forests stretch the lonely heaths where George Borrow (the author of *Lavengro* and *The Romany Rye* which have much to say about the free life of the gipsies he loved) delighted to hear the wind. There are gorse patches and uncanny skeletons of dead trees, and rabbit warrens, and mad March hares. (Hares, 'old Sallies' in East Anglia, were the incarnations of witches, as also were owls.) There are mysterious meres (near Ringmere, probably, the Danes fought the Cambridgeshire Saxons in 1010); and deep pools like the Devil's Punchbowl on Croxton Heath, not always full, due to swallow holes in the chalk beneath. And if you have a map, or hit upon it by lucky chance, you may come to Grimes Graves.

East Anglia is good for sites connected with very early history, and the earliest might well be these ancient flint mines (no giants' graves really) possibly ten thousand years old. In some of the most recent pits you see the chalky galleries where late Stone Age men picked out the flints with oxen's leg bones or red deer antlers. Above, they were chipped into axe heads, scrapers, choppers, hammers; or leaf-shaped and chisel-edged arrow heads, polished knives, curved sickles. Many axe heads were sent off along Peddars Way and Icknield Way unfinished, to be perfected by their new owners. The finds of these worked flint tools in layers of the earth which help to date the remotest history of man, and of the Ice Ages in relation to man, have made East Anglia uniquely important to geologists and archaeologists. To us, they give a sobering view of continuity: 'knappers' (flint-workers) still pursue their craft at Brandon, and strangely enough, still make weapons – but gun-flints, nowadays. And some East Anglian builders can still split, shape and lay flints, and cobbles; for flint (except in the carrstone district near Sandringham) is their local material, and in flint, previously, most of the cottages, walls and barns were built; great churches and guildhalls too, often decorated with pleasing patterns of split and quartered flints and corners of closely packed chippings, called flush work. Grey-blue, cold, hard and sharp as East Anglian winds and skies, flint has a character proper to these parts.

Two thousand years later, the people of East Anglia (Belgic Celts from Europe) were using iron and other metals, for weapons, tools and ornaments. In war time they gathered in hill-forts, high sites often with a double bank and ditch for protection. Go to Warham Camp, lying in a loop of the River Stiffkey near Wighton, Norfolk, to imagine it. (Local people call it the 'Danish Camp', but it is undoubtedly much older than the Danish invasions.) The dominant tribe here would be the Iceni, whose queen when the Romans came was Boudicca, who later led her peoples south in rebellion and burnt Roman Colchester. She might be wearing, as an heirloom, just such a decorated golden collar as lucky tractor-drivers have turned up in 'Goldfield' at Ken Hill, Snettisham; part of hoards hidden, perhaps in an emergency, by a metal-smith. The best Snettisham torcs are in the British Museum, but Norwich Castle has some.

Tamed eventually by the Romans, the Iceni and their descendants settled down to four hundred years or so of (on the whole) beneficial colonial rule: and their chief market town and place of government was Venta Icenorum, or Caistor-by-Norwich, now a great square field of quiet ploughland, sloping down gently to a river. You can walk round the considerable remains of its walls, built of flint and rubble in about A.D. 200. First a village of huts, by A.D. 100 it had a forum, a basilica and public baths. We walked round Venta Icenorum in hot April sun, searching (especially where rabbits and our dog had been at work) for tangible reminders of the life of this once busy place, now so still. We found bases of vases, bits of red Samian ware and Roman tile, and a fragment of burnt, coagulated stuff which *might* be a relic of Caistor's glass industry which flourished about A.D. 300.

By the late three hundreds, Roman hold was wavering, and they may already have brought in Angle mercenaries from north Europe to help defend Caistor and other places against the Saxon pirates in the North Sea. What they had certainly done was to build along the 'Saxon shore' a series of huge forts. From the high walls of Burgh Castle (Gariannonum) which still stands overlooking Breydon Water behind Great Yarmouth, the garrison spotted the raiders and sent warships to destroy them, or used its cavalry to round up those who slipped ashore.

But it was a losing battle and the barbarians came, Angles, Saxons, Jutes. Perhaps when some rich Romano–British family fled westwards or seawards from their villa near the Icknield Way, they buried the spectacular Roman silver dish and household silver found at Mildenhall in Suffolk and now in the British Museum. And who flung up those huge ditch-and-rampart obstructions, facing southwest, which straddle the Icknield Way (now the Newmarket–London road), as if to check the advance of anyone coming up from the west? You can walk along both the Fleam Dyke and the Devil's Dyke (indeed, get a grandstand view of racing on Newmarket Heath from the second) and wonder if it was the newcomers, the Anglo-Saxons, making good their withdrawal into East Anglian fens from the resurgent Romano-British, who had defeated them (under the leader identified with Arthur) at *Mons Badonicus* in about A.D. 500. Whoever made them (and perhaps it was the other side) they are monumental earthworks.

Meanwhile there had arrived into the sandlings of southeast Suffolk some people called the Wuffings, who subdued all the other Anglo-Saxon immigrants of East Anglia, and whose king, Raedwald, was overlord of all southern England. The Wuffings had their royal cemetery at Sutton Hoo, on the east bank of the Deben Estuary. Here, in 1939, was uncovered, beneath an oval ship-barrow, the outline of a great, open rowing vessel. Amidships had been a gabled cabin, collapsed upon the richest, most varied grave goods of this period yet to be found in Europe, unrobbed: jewellery of solid gold crusted with garnets, a wrought-iron standard, a giant sceptre, golden harness, drinking-horns, buckets, bronze and silver bowls, a six-stringed lyre in a beaver-skin bag (I have heard played a reconstructed lyre like it) and much more, which is in the British Museum. But if you visit those quiet barrows at Sutton Hoo, you can imagine where men dragged the burdened boat up from the river, as a memorial to a missing king (for there was no body). And in the Anglo-Saxon poem *Beowulf* you will find descriptions of similar treasure and of feasting in Saxon halls to the music of the harpist. Early Saxon villages are hard to find, since they were built mainly of wood, but some have been excavated in East Anglia, at Mucking in Essex and West Stow in Suffolk, and the sunken huts, the halls and other buildings traced by the pattern of their post-holes. At North Elmham was found a Saxon water cistern, its wooden lining timbers preserved by the water, only an exceptionally dry summer revealing them. And while we dug for Saxon huts and rubbish pits, men were digging pipelines a few hundred yards away to bring the gas from under the North Sea, from those newly-discovered deposits of gas – and oil – in layers so ancient as to make Saxon England seem recent.

So the Saxons, peace-loving farmers, become 'the natives', and the Viking Northmen invade. At Maldon in Essex you can see the probable place – the causeway from Northey Island in Blackwater River – where in A.D. 991 Byrtnoth, Earl of the East Saxons, rashly let the Northmen cross to the mainland and was cut to pieces amidst the flower of his Essex warriors. The poem of *The Battle of Maldon* tells the story.

Byrtnoth's body was buried at Ely, where the monks loved him: and this fenland cathedral is now one of the loveliest in East Anglia, standing up on its little hill surrounded by flat miles much of which in those days must have been marsh or fen. King Cnut, our Danish king (for eventually the Northmen, to some extent, conquered) came to Ely by boat, and heard the monks' chant coming over the water.

The conquering Normans (only, after all, a later generation of 'Northmen') built great fortified dwellings, the castles. My favourite in Norfolk is Castle Rising, a splendid keep standing inside a high grass rampart, the great hall now open to the sky. One day in the late 1420s, some burghers of Norwich came trotting up the slope to the gatehouse. Up the magnificent entrance stairway they tramped, carrying a golden coronet set with pearls and rubies, which King Henry V had pawned to the cities of Norwich and Lynn in exchange for a war loan years ago, before the victory of Agincourt. They handed it over, in the great hall perhaps, to the king's executors (for he had died in 1422) and got in exchange only *some* of the money they had lent. (Whether Lynn ever had its share does not seem clear: there was great rivalry between the two cities.) This quiet scene makes the past of Castle Rising more real to me than many other more dramatic ones.

At Orford, where the wonderful castle built by Henry II guards the Suffolk coast, fishermen once caught a wild man of the sea. Covered with hair, he had no fish tail, though he is called a merman. He was evidently a fine swimmer, for after being imprisoned some time, 'he secretly fled to the sea and was never afterwards seen'.

The Normans were also great builders of churches and monasteries (larger, richer, more widespread than the Saxons, but by no means were the monks more devoted or artistically accomplished). There is enough of Castle Acre Priory left for you to imagine the calm, planned life of these Carthusian monks. You can also see, off the Rere Dorter (dormitory), a row of garde-robes (lavatories) built over a drain running into the River Nar – good water-borne sanitation. One of the oldest memories of medieval monasticism in East Anglia, though with not much to see but a wonderful gateway, is Bury St Edmunds, where the Saxon saint, King Edmund, was finally brought. (He had been shot by the Danes' arrows and beheaded in A.D. 870 at Hellesdon outside Norwich.) Here in the late twelfth century lived a monk called Jocelin of Brakelond, whose chronicle is the most living picture we have of monks getting on together, and of how they ran the town and their huge estates.

Perhaps the most frequented English shrine, however, was that to 'Our Lady of Walsingham'. The little town was often called the 'Holy Land' of Walsingham, because its foundress saw a vision of the house where the angel Gabriel came to Mary in Nazareth, and was told to make one like it as the shrine for a statue of the Mother and Child. From all over England and Europe, ordinary people, as well as kings and queens, made pilgrimage here. The Milky Way itself, stretched in the sky, was said to lead here. And when Ophelia (in

Shakespeare's *Hamlet*) sings the snatch of folk song about the pilgrim:

> 'How should I your true love know
> From another one?
> By his cockle hat and staff
> And his sandal shoon.'

the Elizabethan tune normally used appears in modern hymn books called 'Walsingham'. Now people again go on pilgrimages here.

The city of Norwich has preserved its old and designed its new as well as any other cathedral town in England. In rebuilding, it has isolated numerous pieces of the old city walls. Its castle is one of the finest Norman keeps in England or France, and has an imaginatively displayed museum and a collection of those loving depictions of the Norfolk country and seashore done in the early nineteenth century by Cotman and Crome, and their followers, the Norwich School. The miraculous blue skies or the wild stormy clouds of Cotman's water colours show how he must have loved his 'rare and beautiful Norfolk' as he called it. Crome's pictures of boats, creeks and harbours, in rich browns, sands, and duns, his brooding summer trees and cornfields, invite you to walk back into them. Constable produces the same ache of nostalgia for his unspoilt Suffolk, the Stour country between Sudbury and the sea. Son of a miller of East Bergholt, he grew up with the mill-pools, rivers, trees, cottages and church towers, the wagons and the farm equipment, of this unspectacular yet lovable country he painted, and above all its skies. 'Those scenes made me a painter and I am grateful,' he said. Many of his paintings are in the National Gallery.

Norwich Cathedral, with its Norman tower from which soars up the spire added in 1361, has been since Norman times the centre of the East Anglian bishops (which was first at North Elmham, then at Thetford) and was also a monastery. (In the cloister, look for nine shallow holes on one of the stone benches, where monks played innocent games of nine men's morris. I think you tried to get three marbles in a row, and to stop your opponent doing likewise. An ancestor of noughts and crosses perhaps.) And if you go in by the west gate, given by Sir Thomas Erpingham, the old knight of Agincourt, who kneels in his niche (he has just been cleaned), think of him, as the words he had carved there in 1420 seem to ask. At the top of Elm Hill, the ancient, cobbled street which runs up from Tombland, stands a tall, narrow house called the Briton Arms dating from about 1390. It evidently escaped burning when a fire swept the Dominican friary beyond it in 1413. The flint Guildhall belongs to the fifteenth century too, and so does the best church in Norwich, St Peter Mancroft, overlooking the market with its candy-striped stall-awnings. Norwich has had music festivals since 1770, and at St Peter's Parson Woodforde heard Handel's 'new' opera (new anyway to him), *Judas Maccabaeus*, in 1788. Here, too, is the memorial to Sir Thomas Browne, the gentle physician of Norwich, who tended his patients, wrote his books, and filled his house with curiosities and his garden with flowers and creatures. He wrote, in 1635, the testament of his faith, *Religio Medici*, full of curious, profound wisdom. The Madder Market (where, no doubt, rose-madder for dyeing was sold to the wool trade) has been a theatre in the Elizabethan style for forty years or so. Strangers' Hall (it must have had to do with Dutch or Flemish weavers, usually called 'the Strangers') is a lovely, early Tudor town house, each room now furnished in a different period. There is a collection of old toys and dolls' houses, and in the cellar, shop and trade signs, and old vehicles. The renovated Assembly House, with its ornate plaster ceilings and glittering candelabra, is just as pleasingly of the eighteenth century. The twentieth has given the City Hall (fine, but sadly dwarfing St Peter's) and the more recent new library with its miles of ingenious shelving space.

At King's Lynn you are within sound and scent of the quayside, where the River Ouse runs out into the Wash and where ships have come in and gone out for a thousand years. Ancient warehouses (many being refurbished), the pilot's house with its red-brick look-out, the handsome Customs House built about 1683, and the two basins with their modern cranes, petroleum storage tanks, and roll-on roll-off terminal, show the port's long history. The town's heart is the elegant Tuesday Market Place: between here and Nelson Street you pass centuries of history, including two medieval guildhalls, and Hampton Court, fifteenth-century headquarters of the Hanseatic merchants – all restored and used. Lynn was noted for wine-importing from medieval times until very recently. Grain she has always handled; but that main import of earlier centuries, coal, has given place in bulk to petroleum products. Timber, iron and steel come in too. Lynn's expanding new industries, food processing, ball bearings and many others (more valuable but less colourful than her one-time merry-go-round making) give work to an increasing population, all eyes on Europe. In 1643, when most of East Anglia was Puritan and Cromwellian, gallant little Lynn held out for King Charles I for five weeks, being blockaded by the Parliamentary navy. This adds significance to the brooding statue of Charles II above the Customs House door. King's Lynn has a flourishing annual arts festival, centred upon the restored Guildhall of St George, which is very lively and local, supported by painters, actors and musicians from nearby, and those from the larger festival at Aldeburgh.

An early lover of Aldeburgh was Edward Fitzgerald who translated the *Rubáiyát* of Omar Khayyám. This lovable man lived at Woodbridge in the 1850s, where he would be seen about in a cape, a hat, and bare feet in summer. Both Tennyson and Thackeray referred to him as their best friend. He was happiest in his little boat 'round the coast to Aldborough, with some bottled porter, some bread and cheese and some good rough soul who works the boat . . .' A less happy poet, William Cowper, died in East Dereham, Norfolk: he was a gentle, religious poet but a melancholy man, even though we may remember him by the racy ballad of John Gilpin, whose horse ran away with him from London to Ware. George Borrow was born near Dereham, at a place with the delightful name of Dumpling Green. Dickens never lived in East Anglia, but he stayed here: and it is an odd thing that if anyone says 'Yarmouth' to me, I see not that long, modern stretch of built-up, glittering, neon-lit entertainment, but Mr Peggotty's house, the upturned boat on the foreshore, where David Copperfield used to stay. At Langham near the north Norfolk coast lived Captain Marryat, who had served in the Royal Navy before he took to writing novels of sea life like *Mr Midshipman Easy*. At Ditchingham lived Henry Rider Haggard, the author of that enthralling story, *King Solomon's Mines*. Robert Louis Stevenson, travelling in Suffolk (and used to the plainer villages of the north) saw the beautiful little town of Long Melford at a remove from life (as writers often do, when a place catches their imagination) and described its 'great screens of trees that seem twice as high as trees should seem, and everything else like what it ought to be in a novel'. From the quietness of his Suffolk parish of Wetheringsett, the imagination of the Elizabethan Richard Hakluyt ranged over the oceans and the new world, as he enlarged his famous work, the *Principall Navigations, Voiages and Discoveries of the English Nation*. Of modern writers, the most memorable may well be the Norfolk historian, R. W. Ketton Cremer, whose knowledge of Norfolk people and affairs, particularly in the seventeenth and eighteenth centuries, was unsurpassed, but who wrote his books with such lightness and charm that you do not have to be an historian to enjoy them.

Aldeburgh Festival, the creation of the composer Benjamin Britten and a group of like-minded musicians, arose from his avowed dependence on his native place for inspiration. In America, as a young man, he found a copy of the eighteenth-century poet George Crabbe (who lived at Aldeburgh) and read the story of Peter Grimes in Crabbe's narrative poem, *The Borough*. Britten realized then that he must put down his own roots. 'I belong at home – there – in Aldeburgh. I have tried to bring music *to* it . . . and all the music I write comes *from* it.' Certainly the opera *Peter Grimes* came from it – from the sea whose waves in winter Crabbe describes:

> 'Curl'd as they come, they strike with furious force,
> And then, re-flowing, take their grating course,
> Raking the rounded flints . . .'

If you have ever joined in *Let's Make an Opera* you will know how local too is this story of the little sweep. When the festival's new concert hall, built out of the Maltings at Snape, was burned down in 1970, Mozart's opera *Idomeneo* (a story set in a Greek sea-town) took place in Blythburgh church instead. The singers were doubtless keyed up by the catastrophe and the sudden difficulties, and the result was a breathtaking performance. When Neptune arose from beneath the sea, I found myself shivering as if in the numinous presence of some real old sea-god.

So you always get back to the powerful, timeless sea, in East Anglia, the huddled, cobbled villages facing northeasterly gales, their rows of cottages backing on to the blast. Inland it is still possible, on a May afternoon as you come upon a few flint houses round a green, with hawthorn hedges white as junket, to feel as if you are in the times when a dragon may loom up pursued by a knight; or a 'woodwose' (a wild man) like the one carved on a beam in the Bull Inn at Long Melford, peer out at you from a thicket. Remoteness, in England, is a vanishing beauty, but she still has a few citadels in East Anglia.

A GHOST OF LONDON

by Leon Garfield

A signpost has but one good arm: the one that points to London. Other arms seem trumpery and unnecessary; for who, given a choice, would take any road but the highway to London? The country may have its dubious charms – its quaint churches with crooked spires, its sleepy woods and fields and village streets as dozy as its churchyards; but no matter what the occasion, when a man travels outwards from London and sees a sign pointing back to the Town, he feels, in his heart of hearts, that he's going the wrong way.

And so he is; but he'll come back again, even if only as a ghost. The other day I saw an uncle of mine crossing the road at Notting Hill Gate where the traffic roars and rages, stinks and fumes and creeps selfishly into an almighty mess. He was a small man, my uncle, but well filled out and with hair of so clean a silver that I could have sworn it was hall-marked. I stopped; I trembled; my eyes filled with disbelieving tears. My uncle had been dead these fifteen years.

Though not born in London, my uncle was a Londoner by habit of love. I would have said by adoption, but my uncle was not the sort of man to be adopted. He was a connoisseur – an admirer – a great experiencer of life.

As I watched, he walked rapidly through the traffic and made for the Portobello Road. I hurried after him and presently found myself among the tilting confusion of stalls, bazaars and grimy shops overflowing the pavements with ancient articles – all priceless inasmuch as one would be hard put to say what they were worth.

Chamber pots, paintings, brass candlesticks – and there was my uncle, stroking the varnished neck of an enormous gilded roundabout horse! I ran across the road and into the shop, but he'd gone and I was trapped by the dealer – an old character actor who'd exchanged one world of makebelieve for another.

At first he made several attempts to sell me something – a painting, a chipped lustre teapot, a spoon . . .

'Do you believe in ghosts?' I asked distractedly, looking up and down the crowded street for a glimpse of good silver hair among the brass and plate.

'We are all ghosts,' said the retired actor, amiably resigned to selling no more than himself. 'How many, do you suppose, of those people out there would freeze the blood of their friends if they saw them? How many of them are really unrecognized ghosts?'

'At least one,' I murmured.

'When I was in the Theatre Royal at Drury Lane,' went on the actor, 'playing Polonius on the very boards where Garrick stormed, I saw the Gentleman in Grey. He came in quietly at the back of the circle. He was middle-sized, wearing a long grey riding cloak, a powdered wig and carrying a three-cornered hat. He wore a sword which I could just make out under his cloak. He was rather handsome and looked a little like old Sir George Alexander – whom you wouldn't remember, which is your loss, my friend, for he was a great actor – but it wasn't the ghost of dear George. He smiled down at the stage as politely as kiss-your-hand, then he sat in an empty place . . . the only empty seat in the house, I might say. "This above all, to thine own self be true," I began; when he stood up, bowed – and vanished into thin air. Several times after that I saw him, but only at matinées. He never came at night, having other engagements, I suppose. Some say he's the ghost of an old-time playgoer who cannot bear to miss a good performance; but others think the truth of him is more sinister. A hundred or more years ago when the house was being done up, some workmen came upon a hollow wall in the upper circle on the Russell Street side. They broke it down and found a small room behind it. And in that dusty room, tumbled in the rubble on the floor, was the skeleton of a young man with a dagger lying among his ribs. Most likely he was some country youth, robbed and murdered and tidied away. He's buried now in the churchyard on the corner of Russell Street, and is believed to be the unquiet spirit who haunts the matinées at Drury Lane. But whenever I saw him, he never looked vengeful or gloomy. He always looked remarkably well-pleased with my performance, and I came to take his appearance as quite a compliment from a gentleman who must have seen Garrick.

'He was,' went on the talkative antique actor, 'a true London ghost. For London ghosts, in my experience, are none of your ghastly nuns or hanged monks. They are cheerful ladies and gentlemen of the day before yesterday who cannot bear to leave the Town – even for heaven.'

Certainly this was a view of ghosts that took in my uncle. I caught sight of him again, neatly dressed in a grey suit with, appropriately enough, invisible checks. He was fingering part of a Staffordshire tea-set that pretended to be Derby, (a sort of thick-eared sheep in wolf's clothing), and smiling most knowledgeably.

He'd been in the antique line himself, though he was more of a cracked plate and Welsh dresser man than your gaudy Kensington Chippendaler. He conducted a business, for a short time, near the Angel at Islington, and had one of the best collections of forged china marks in the whole of London. This wasn't by any means intentional on his part; he seemed to have an instinct for them. I always remember him as being a tremendous authority on china marks, and many was the cream cake or cup of tea he'd spilled in a private effort to see what might be printed underneath . . .

My uncle loved Islington, and always said it was the healthiest spot in London. Not two hundred years ago, he used to tell me, it was known as 'the London Hospital', as it was so famous for invalids recovering from the busy Town. There used to be a story told by the great Dr Hunter of an old lady sent by her physician to take lodgings in Islington to mend her declining health. She agreed to a suite of rooms near the Angel, but, on coming down the stairs, saw that the banisters were cracked and broken. 'Before I come,' she said to the landlord, 'these must be repaired.' 'Madam,' said the landlord, 'it would serve no purpose as the undertaker's men, in bringing down the coffins, are continually breaking the banisters.' The lady paled, gathered her skirts, and returned to the perils of the Town where coffins were more discreet – and less frequent.

My uncle, as luck would have it, died in Brighton – if such a gentle fading away as his could have been called dying. I think he must have been very distressed to find himself lying in provincial soil. Although he was second to none in his admiration for the countryside – frequently making somewhat grand excursions down the river and commenting knowledgeably on field and foliage, cheese and pickles and quaint inn signs – he always maintained that the countryside was but the Londoner's garden. 'And who,' he would ask, looking exceedingly dapper, 'wants to *live* in a garden?'

I don't know when he came out of his Brighton grave, but it must have been with a rush and a sigh, followed by a hasty flitting up the Queen's Road to the station and catching the old Brighton Belle by the wispy skin of his gold-capped teeth. Then to London!

Perhaps that very morning I saw him was his first one out...? I nearly caught up with him at the china stall in the Portobello Road; but he seemed to know he was pursued, for he hurried up a side street to Holland Park Avenue where I saw him swing on to a crowded bus with all the agility of a City man born and bred.

I caught the bus following and saw my uncle get off at Marble Arch where he skipped across the wide, furious road as recklessly as only a ghost dared. Not wanting to join him in spirit, so to speak, I waited for the traffic to snarl into its usual halt. As I stood on the corner of Edgware Road, I saw him walking along Tyburn Way where he paused momentarily to stare down at that dreadful place in the road where the gallows once stood. Then he looked up with a deeply serious expression as if he, with his phantom eyes, could see the swinging forest of dead men's feet.

Eight times a year were hanging days, and all the journeymen and apprentices made them public holidays so that businesses were forced to close as their workmen had gone to watch the hanging.

Nearby, in Hyde Park itself, where lovers stroll and speakers rant, was that other execution ground – for the soldiery. My uncle used to tell me a story of a nursemaid – in the days when there were nursemaids – who was ogled every morning by a handsome red-coated soldier in a deep blue cloak. He always sat on the same bench, as if waiting for her to pass by; and when she did, he'd jump to his feet, salute first her and then the infant in the pram – who, I believe, was my uncle himself. He never addressed a word to her; just saluted and flashed his eyes. One day she could bear it no longer and asked the warrior outright what his intentions were. She feared he was already married, with a large family at Woolwich, maybe, and only meant to trifle with her. Even then he didn't answer, so angrily she pulled at his cloak. It fell aside and revealed his chest, blackened with a dozen musket holes. It seemed the bench on which he sat had been placed on the very spot where he'd been executed long ago. The nursemaid and my uncle never passed that way again.

The traffic had knitted itself to a standstill; only bicycles moved. I began to cross when I saw my uncle's lively spectre nip across the top of Park Lane and weave his way down Oxford Street where once the hangman's cart came rumbling; 'going West,' as they said at Newgate Gaol of condemned men setting out in their last direction.

I hastened in his wake and glimpsed him, through the sauntering, shopping crowds, looking quizzically up at what was new and shaking his bright silver head. In no time at all he'd reached Bond Street and he was all gold-toothed smiles. Bond Street held a special place in his heart. He was, in all his many heydays, a Bond Street stroller. He bought his tie-pins there, and his smart grey hats with curly brims. His umbrellas and walking sticks came from Bond Street . . . but he himself never had a business there. If he had, I think it would have spoiled it for him. In Bond Street, he always said, a gentleman buys, he doesn't sell. I saw him loitering under the shabby archway of Sotheby's, the auctioneers, where he loved to go and sit through breathtaking sales of masterpieces, marking down impossible prices in his catalogue. He used to collect these catalogues and I always imagined the paintings had actually passed through his hands instead of only through his mind.

All this was when he presided over a business in Shaftesbury Avenue. I thought he was going that way, for he turned abruptly, went along Maddox Street, crossed Regent Street and plunged, with a sophisticated smile, into Soho.

I felt a sudden pang of sadness when I glimpsed that smile. I remembered it so well in life. It appeared whenever Soho was mentioned. There was something secret about my uncle's Soho . . . as indeed there is about every Londoner's Soho. It is a strange, seedy, fairytale country inside the Town. Its very air is different, being heavy with a complicated smell of cooking. Its narrow streets twist and turn and double back on themselves with an air of cunning surprise. Promising thoroughfares dwindle and end unnaturally in the silent backs of warehouses that have no fronts with nothing in sight but an interrupted cat. Then one sidles through an alleyway (that was certainly not there a moment ago) into a teeming street where dark-eyed Latins slink furtively from corner to corner as if pursued by invisible policemen or wives.

Magazine and bookshops bloom in cultured profusion and are fairly stuffed with pictures of ladies with no clothes on; and next door to them are premises where, for a modest sum, ladies may be seen taking their clothes off to music. All in all Soho is very like the Garden of Eden before the Tree of Knowledge was broached: fig-leaves are only used for cooking.

But my uncle's secret was something else altogether. In the springtime of the year he would put on a grey top hat, grey morning suit and hang a pair of expensive leather-sleeved binoculars round his neck like an amulet. Then he'd go, jaunty in the sunshine, to his bookmaker in Frith Street (Thrift Street in the old days) and wager small fortunes on the fate of horses running in the misty distance over Epsom Downs. Although he'd never been to an actual race-course in his life, he knew to the last blade of grass the condition of the turf, and would look critically at the Soho weather and pronounce on every horse's chance.

Surprisingly enough, with all his knowledge, he never won; but he took his losses like a gentleman. He always believed that there was something peculiarly gentlemanly about losing; our family, on the other hand, thought there was something peculiarly uncle-ish about it.

He loved to talk of the great days of Soho when it was fashionable and when Soho Square was bounded by elegance and beauty . . . and when gambling in Thrift Street was so very gentlemanly that a noble lord, losing fifty thousand guineas on the turn of a single card, could nod to his companion and say: 'Damned fortunate I wasn't playing deep, eh?'

Lord Camelford was a gentleman my uncle would have admired. In 1804 he fought a duel in Kensington with a certain Captain Best. Now this duel had arisen foolishly and anyone but a great gentleman like Lord Camelford would have withdrawn and been glad of it. But because Captain Best was known to be the finest shot in England, the upright lord 'was fearful lest his reputation should suffer if he made any concession, however slight, to such a person'.

He lies in St Anne's Church, Soho, with his coronet on his coffin and a bullet in his breast. His heart was true to the end; it was only his head that was a little shaky.

Next door to him sleeps King Theodore of Corsica, 'who died in this parish, December 11th 1756, immediately after leaving the King's Bench Prison by the benefit of the Act of Insolvency; in consequence of which he registered his kingdom of Corsica for the benefit of his creditors.' Alas! poor king; his history was even more tangled than my uncle's. I think there are few things sadder than the description of his end. As soon as he'd been released from prison 'he took a sedan chair and went to the Portuguese minister; but not finding him at home, and not having a sixpence to pay, he desired the chairmen to carry him to a tailor in Soho, whom he prevailed upon to harbour him; but he fell sick the next day, and died in three more. So he went to the place that levels kings and beggars; an unnecessary journey for him who had already fallen from one to the other.' It was the tradesmen who harboured him and who'd known him in his royalty who paid for his burial.

What a melancholy sight it must have been! And all the more so for not being high tragedy such as might have become a king. Sick, bewildered and penniless . . . and facing his last enemies in the persons of two burly London chairmen.

* * *

'And what might this be?'

I started. A taxi driver was leaning out of his cab and staring with effortless insolence at a foreign coin that a passenger had just given him.

'Come out of a cracker, did it?'

The passenger, standing on the pavement in Dean Street, blushed furiously and answered in some language that was not English. I fancied the earth about St Anne's Church shuddered as King Theodore stirred in sympathy. The passenger – a lean and swarthy man who'd doubtless faced Corsican bandits and Parisian gendarmes and subdued them – quailed before the merciless wit of this spiritual descendant of the London chairmen.

A smallish crowd had gathered. A car, trapped behind the halted taxi, hooted piteously. Slowly the taxi driver looked round. The impatient driver shrank behind his wheel . . .

'You're 'olding up the traffic, guv'nor,' said the taxi driver reproachfully to his passenger who was now struggling with a purse and spilling money into the street. Suddenly the taxi driver beamed. He reached out and took a coin from his passenger's fingers and returned the offending first one.

'That's all I want, guv.,' he said amiably. The crowd began to drift away with a vague sense of disappointment that no blood had been shed; the poor wretch, doubtless filled with hatred for London and Londoners, was on his hands and knees gathering up his money. A small boy began to help him, and, apparently himself; for the taxi driver, in no hurry, remarked protectively, ''oppit, lad! Or I'll call a copper!'

Then, just as he was about to slam the cab door and drive off to free the accumulated traffic behind him, a gentleman nipped neatly inside and gave him directions. It was the ghost of my uncle.

I caught sight of his face; he was staring at me with a curiously mischievous smile. A feeling of annoyance overcame me. Plainly he knew I was pursuing him. Why then was he being so tantalizing? He and I had always got along very well. He always led me to believe I was his favourite nephew. The taxi drove off, and with enormous good fortune I found another almost directly to follow it. We drew alongside at the traffic lights at Cambridge Circus, but my uncle steadfastly refused to meet my eye . , . however, his smile continued mischievous.

The traffic lights changed and the taxis moved on towards Long Acre and Covent Garden. The great market-place was empty; only a few corpses of oranges and the ghostly smell of cabbage lingered on. Posters for Wagner and Richard Strauss were displayed outside the Opera House. There was something overripe everywhere.

Once my uncle talked my mother into letting him take me to 'The Garden' at the weird hour of half-past four in the morning. At first my mother flew into a righteous panic. She thought he meant Hatton Garden, where the great diamond dealers live in musty houses behind brass grills. For in those days my uncle was in the jewellery line and was always selling the Russian Crown Jewels – or something very like them. God knows what my mother imagined we would be up to in Hatton Garden in the dark. Perhaps she fancied we were setting out on a career of crime? Certainly she hadn't much faith in my uncle's ability to succeed in anything else. But when she understood that he meant Covent Garden and the market, she calmed down and nodded resignedly when my uncle said it would be 'educational'.

'Educational' was his favourite word, and, although he used it pretty broadly, I think the meaning *he* gave it was a good deal truer than many a schoolteacher's notion.

It was bitterly cold that black morning when he and I set out. He wouldn't hear of taking sandwiches and vacuum flasks; the Nag's Head in Floral Street was the place for early nourishment. In the old days, he informed me, with that reminiscent, knowledgeable air he wore so well, strolling players used to encumber the Nag's Head, muttering their lengths of forty-two lines in the hope of attracting the manager of some travelling company short of an actor.

My uncle was wonderfully well-stocked with such oddments of 'education', though how many of them he'd invented to keep his standing with a child I will never know. London street names fascinated him as they recalled, in their haunting greenness and grimness, the Town's tortuous past. Sometimes he'd murmur them like a rosary: 'Whitefriars . . . Blackfriars, Newgate and Aldgate; Cripplegate . . . Fetter Lane, Ave Maria Lane, Godliman Street, Threadneedle Street . . .'

'Why Cripplegate?' I'd ask him. 'Because,' said he, 'in olden times lamed men once threw away their crutches there and walked upright when the body of a martyred king was carried by. Remember that, young man. Such pieces of education will help to make you well-informed. Threadneedle Street, for intance, was where the Merchant Tailors lived and kept a yard engraved on silver to take to Bartholomew Fair once a year.'

I did indeed remember – such items tend to stick in the mind – but I can't say I've used the knowledge to such effect as my uncle did.

Covent Garden, he told me, was once the kitchen garden of the abbot of Westminster before the monasteries were humbled and tumbled by Henry VIII. We reached the market soon after dawn when the lorryloads of fruit and vegetables and flowers from all corners of the kingdom had made a huge, noisy buttonhole in the dim grey suit of the Town. The air was strong with country smells and loud with argument as Kensington greengrocers and Whitechapel housewives fought for the best of the crop. Monstrous vehicles crept through the narrow streets, trumpeting like grandfather elephants in a jungle of bargaining monkeys. My uncle, feeling peckish, struggled to reach the Nag's Head, but then, remembering that I was too young to be allowed inside, generously found a lorryman's café where we had hot bacon sandwiches. He ate his with a real connoisseurship – as if it had been the rarest delicacy – and told me between mouthfuls, that these humble eating-places with their deal tables and peeling walls, were the true inheritors of the old-time coaching inns where men of the road met for regular refreshment. Nowadays the inns had got above themselves and beer was by no means what it used to be. I think he told me this to console me for not having been allowed in the Nag's Head.

We went back to 'The Garden' after that; and my uncle, all shrewdness and commercial wisdom, bought some pineapples. He bought two cases of them. I think he only meant to buy two fruits, but on the way home he explained to me the financial advantage of buying in bulk.

So much for Covent Garden. I saw my uncle's ghost poke its head out of his cab window and smile at the scene of his past triumphs as we passed it by. Then, as if taken with a cramp, his taxi began to twist and weave and turn through ancient narrow streets, baffling cars behind and terrifying those in front. There's a tale told about these streets of a young man, up from the country, carrying a black bag. One winter's night he set out for Portugal Street to find his way to the Strand. He is still looking; and sometimes his misty figure is to be seen, returning to his starting place or else in Clare Market, disconsolately peering about him. No one ever heard of him actually reaching the Strand.

My uncle's taxi trundled on, coming out of the angular confusion of haphazard streets into the grave elegance of Lincoln's Inn Fields – like some tormented legal argument that concludes abruptly in a peaceful settlement. Then into Carey Street where I saw the ghost of my uncle's face go pale enough to frighten itself before it vanished back inside the cab. Carey Street had never held happy memories for him. Though it was kept from me at the time, (it was spoken of in hushed whispers that were swallowed whenever I came into the room so that I concluded everyone had been talking of some misdeed of mine too shameful to confront me with), I discovered afterwards that my uncle had made his début before the Bankruptcy Court. Subsequently, I believe, he gave an encore. I never heard that he went to prison, but if he did I'm sure some fellow prisoner remembered him warmly and benefited from his company.

From my uncle's earliest days he'd been concerned with the law; not the receiving end of it, so to speak, but the other – the working part. He'd been apprenticed to a solicitor – as he liked to describe his clerkship – and he had great ambitions of going into the law line. Once he took me to the office he'd worked in until he'd spread his wings and fled that oddly seedy nest. It was 'somewhere in the City' – down one of those cracks of lanes that had begun, long ago in rural days as a right of way and had come, by legal degrees, to be a wrong of way, full of solicitors as devious as the passages and stairways that led to their rooms. My uncle's office was reached by a lift pulled up by a rope made greasy by countless conniving and desperate hands. It might have been the very rope used at Tyburn on hanging days – it had such a ghastly and final air. Of the office itself I remember little save that the lamps all wore green shades which gave the place an oddly sylvan air and made one think of robbers resting in a forest at night . . .

I don't know how long my uncle was in the law, but he acquired a tremendous fund of knowledge about it and was recognized as the family authority. Even my mother deferred to him on legal matters – so long as they remained academic and no action was required. But I remember there was an aunt of mine – a small, round, owlish woman compounded of righteousness and obstinacy – who was once called for jury service. Naturally my uncle took a keen interest; I think he was also a little jealous, but being the good-natured gentleman he was, he laid his envy aside and entered wholeheartedly into my aunt's duties. The case that she was called upon to hear was at the Old Bailey itself. It was an enormous libel action in which, day after day, famous counsels fought desperate duels of wit which the wise old judge patiently unravelled for the benefit of my aunt and her eleven companions. The case was quite notorious and grew more complicated; but my uncle had the measure of it all. Every night when my aunt came back, my uncle skilfully undermined whatever had been achieved during the day. The consequence of his labours, and my aunt's respect for them, was that the jury failed to reach a verdict. I believe the judge said some harsh things to the jury – which my aunt took personally, as she came home in tears. The case was tried again later – at a cost of many thousands of pounds. My aunt said it served them right.

Now Carey Street and its pale, hurrying figures (no one seems to loiter in Carey Street) were left behind. The taxi turned into Chancery Lane. I saw my uncle point south and gesticulate at the driver who shrugged his shoulders. Having been dead these fifteen years, my uncle didn't know that Chancery Lane was one-way nowadays. I saw him slump back and resign himself to another tangled progress that ended up in Fetter Lane before he found himself aiming south.

I wondered how many other surprises he'd come upon, and how many more changes had baffled him. Women's skirts, soaring skywards, must have opened his critical eyes. I say 'critical' because ever since his Shaftesbury Avenue days when he most mysteriously became proprietor of a modish dress shop, he was apt to pronounce so shrewdly on a woman's shape that my mother refused to have him in the house when we had company. I recall there was one shape in particular that he admired without reservation. Her name was Sandra and she played the accordion in spangled tights at the impossibly grand Astoria Cinema in Finsbury Park (stars moved and twinkled in its roof) between films. He took me round to her dressing-room once, and I was almost overpowered by the smell of powder and greasepaint and the near-to sight of Sandra, forty times more vivid than life. Afterwards we all went back to her flat in Maida Vale which was a kind of Aladdin's cave of stuffed satin pouffes and cushions and shiny standard lamps from Gamage's and Maple's.

Presently we reached Fleet Street and crawled up, through the remorseless traffic, towards the solemn bulk of St Paul's. Glass and granite newpaper buildings towered on the left, and across the street small, teeming shops, like worn-down rotten teeth, admitted gaps between them that slunk down frowsily to the River Thames. Inns, taverns, pubs – all with fantastic names – beckoned from every court and alley and clinked and buzzed with journalists made ghosts before their time. News has been the business of Fleet Street since its beginning . . . even when the Strand was still called Westminster High Street and the walled City, rich and grim, frowned down Ludgate Hill towards the easy frivolity of the palace at Westminster. I think it must have begun even before the businesslike Romans came, when some ancient, ancient Briton, his woad worn to a whisper, sat on the side of Ludgate Hill and idly watched anguished borrowers hastening to and from the fortress of King Lud. He sold the news of these comings and goings – for a goat or a chicken – to the extravagant kingdom down the road, which was always short of money and always hopeful of borrowing it. Then as time went on and this ancient, ancient journalist waxed fat and even older, he enlivened dull August days when men were neither borrowers nor lenders with trifles like 'Famous Druid Dies' and found that passers-by were just as eager to find out which one as ever they'd been to learn the soberer facts of life. Others joined him; rival establishments sprang up – and Fleet Street was born.

We had lost my uncle! The taxi driver turned a baffled face towards me and shrugged his shoulders. The thin and sinuous city lanes about St Paul's had swallowed him up. A thousand taxis moved in all directions, oozing and flowing through what were no more cracks in the grey stone and then seeping away like black blood carrying rosy-faced, bowler-hatted corpuscles to the limbs and vital organs of the City. We crawled down street after street, ever deeper into the City's heart; but it was hopeless. I paid the taxi off in Milton Street – once Grub Street but elevated to remember John Milton who died nearby. They buried him with tremendous honours in St Giles's Church in Cripplegate . . . and later dug him up again and pillaged him for souvenirs. His hair went and five of his teeth were knocked out and distributed to admirers.

I stayed in the City for I don't know how long, scouring the courts and lanes for a sight of my dead uncle. I longed to ask him how my father was, and my mother, too . . . and what line he was in now and if he was doing well and where he bought his suits. I searched for him in the Poultry, where once poultry was actually sold, in Old Jewry, (old indeed: William the Conqueror began it, bringing his rich Jews from Rouen to settle there), along Leadenhall Street and Lombard Street and round about the august Mansion House. A hundred brisk businessmen looked wonderfully like him from behind; but, for all I knew, they might have been the ghosts of other folk's uncles, for none of them turned out to be the ghost of mine.

At last the City began to empty. Suddenly streams of clerks and typists had begun to clog the streets so that it seemed a marvel that the Town had homes for them all. Steadily they squeezed down into the bowels of the earth for trains to roar them off to Barnet and Cockfosters; or surged inside the scarlet dinosaurs of buses to be lumbered away to the wilds of Tottenham Hale or Tooting Bec. Presently the City grew quiet and empty; the huge buildings looked a shade thinner and paler – as in consequence of their violent purging. A small quantity of pink and yellow paper twisted and fluttered in the gutter of Cheapside, like autumnal leaves from a banknote tree. Idly I picked one up. On one side was printed a fragment of an invoice for an unknown quantity of mixed spices, and on the other, scrawled with every semblance of haste as if under the very eye of a sternly suspicious office manager, was 'Gatehouse. 9.30 Love . . .' Here the paper was torn so I never knew who the love was from. I pictured two office juniors, stealthily making their first tryst among mountainous bales of bay leaves and macaroni . . .

I wondered whether the tryst was to be at the Gatehouse in Highgate, which if one can believe a plaque in its dirty red brick, had been a meeting place for close on six hundred years. Certainly some of the regulars always looked to have been waiting for some time . . .

There's a ghost in the Gatehouse; a previous landlord saw it and fell downstairs with fright. But then most London pubs are haunted, as many a landlord will take his Bible oath on. Usually they inhabit small, out of the way, upstairs rooms where long ago they hanged themselves or shot themselves on account of losing their money or the love of a black-eyed barmaid. Noises are heard from the fatal rooms – and sometimes a curious smell of onions frying . . . There's one ghost that cooks toast for breakfast and fills the premises with a delicious smell at 6 o'clock in the morning. But these tavern spectres never intrude on licensing hours. There seems to be some supernatural law that forbids the consumption of spirits by spirits.

The saloon bar of the Gatehouse is a large, dim, slightly oppressive room with a brown pie-crust ceiling so that it seems one is being slowly baked in an enormous steak-and-kidney pie. I sat there from 9 o'clock, feeling gloomy and angry about losing my uncle for a second time in my life. I watched the customers, but, as yet, none of them looked young and romantic enough to have scribbled the note I found in Cheapside. Perhaps, after all, there was another Gatehouse in Clapham or Finsbury Park?

I went up to the bar, prepared for the usual wait to catch the barmaid's endlessly roving eye. To my great surprise, the landlord – who had been deep in conversation with a customer over a counter at the back – came smiling and hurrying to serve me. Without a word he filled a tankard and pushed it towards me. I thanked him and offered the money. He shook his head. Was it the Queen's birthday I wondered?

'Compliments of the gent in the other bar,' he said and jerked his head towards the counter he'd left. I saw my uncle, beaming and twinkling and toasting me in whisky!

'Uncle!' I shouted.

'Time gentlemen please,' said the landlord. 'Drink up, if you please.'

I gulped my beer and ran for the door. I saw him scampering down the Village High Street, weaving in and among the customers disgorded from the Prince of Wales, the Angel, the Rose and Crown, and the Duke's Head. Highgate is a nourishing place. Then as the hill dipped down, he paused and surveyed the wide, dark carpet of London laid out in winking lights before him. I almost caught up with him, but he glanced at his watch and made off again at high speed. Now began a chase of extraordinary dimensions as I pursued the ghost of my uncle on foot and by variable bus across the night-time Town. Insistently the memory of a fairy tale haunted my mind, and I wondered where the ghost had to be by midnight. Was there a carriage awaiting him somewhere – a great dark affair with phantom horses and a smell of graves?

As we rushed southward through streets of darkness and then abruptly into little clusterings of light and life I began to feel that the Town itself was composed of ghosts – the ghosts of villages joined together by acres of brick nothingness . . . every village still with its own high street – even its own newspaper – and then road upon road with green names that ached to be grassy again.

We crossed Trafalgar Square where the fountains blazed silver and Nelson brooded among the stars. Big Ben, suspended in the night like God's yellow pocket watch, showed twenty to twelve. My uncle raced down Whitehall, across Parliament Square and into Victoria Street. He hailed a taxi and caught it – ghosts have the most extraordinary luck – and left me to follow on foot. I got to Victoria Station at a minute to twelve. My uncle's carriage was standing at the platform, but the ticket collector had already closed the gates. Helplessly I stared across the bars and my uncle waved to me from a first class carriage window. Then the last train back to Brighton began to move and soon to dwindle away. I wondered how many other ghosts were playing cards with him as they all went back to their provincial graves. I turned away, sadly at first, back to the night-time Town. And then I remembered the one-time actor in Portobello Road who'd talked so eloquently and comfortingly of ghosts.

I walked more briskly now, making my way towards Hyde Park Corner, passing uncles galore.

'Buy an apple, sir?'

Who said that? Could it have been the ghost of the old apple seller whose stall, scarce two hundred years ago, used to mark the spot where, after passing the Knightsbridge turnpike, London proper began?

AN ANCIENT PLACE

by Penelope Lively

Just behind the village of Leafield, in the Windrush Valley, there is a prehistoric barrow, a small lumpy hill crowned with trees. Climb to the top of it and you are at the highest point for miles around, standing in the centre of a great bowl of English landscape. It is the ordered, hand-made landscape of midland England – as ancient as Wychwood Forest below there to the east, a remnant of the green tide that once covered all this, and as new as the giant pylons striding up from Berkshire, or the VC10s that lumber down the sky to Brize Norton, looming like huge grey ghosts over the Buttercross in Witney. It is a landscape of elm and willow, ridged with dark hedges: horizons packed with trees; stone villages under huge skies of heaped English clouds; small rivers with lovely names, Evenlode and Windrush; churches, quarries, farms. Its variety is enormous: river valleys like the Windrush – private and withdrawn, a place apart; bleak uplands beyond Chipping Norton, hamlets in forgotten pockets of land, thriving towns like Witney, industrial Oxford at one corner, Roman Cirencester at another. To find a unity you must ignore county boundaries, leave out the Thames Valley, which is another place altogether, or the Berkshire Downs to the south, and look north, up to Warwick, where another part of midland England begins, different again. Here, in a rough triangle, is a piece of landscape as old as human existence, recording in each field, each road, each group of buildings, the story of how people have used the place and marked it for ever with the evidence of that use. For this is in no way a natural landscape. It has its rivers, its contours, and the rock and soil that have dictated what could be done with it – all the rest is made by hand, painfully and patiently, over a couple of thousand years. The fields come largely from the eighteenth-century enclosures, with everywhere the long backbones of medieval ridge and furrow to recall an earlier agricultural economy. The road systems preserve Saxon boundaries, and tortuous medieval tracks, and local drove roads and salt ways and here and there ancient, prehistoric routes and long straight snatches of Roman road. Towns like Burford and Witney and Chipping Norton and the fine fourteenth- and fifteenth-century churches are a legacy of the sheep that grew fat on Cotswold grass, and the medieval merchants who grew fat on Cotswold wool. The last hundred years contribute the wide slash of new roads and the new estates that spill out into the country from old towns and villages.

A landscape made by people. A people whose descendants are, by and large, still here. What they do has changed, and how they live has changed out of all recognition in the last fifty years, but they are still born and die in places where their names will be scattered through three or four hundred years of parish registers in the local church. We are a permanent people, the English. Rooted, static. I live in a village where, fifty years ago, everyone living in the place also worked there. But the tractor came, and the car, and now three or four farms have replaced a couple of dozen, ten men work land that once needed scores, and the village looks away, to Witney or to Oxford, for services it used to do without, or provide for itself. But the same people still live here. They make cars now, or build houses, instead of farming the land: they may travel twenty miles a day to work, but they still live in the same place, and I daresay their children will do the same. Only the old people preserve the memory of the simple economic reasons that once kept people here – the specialists, the men who were shepherds or blacksmiths or hedgers or pig-slaughterers, occupations for which there is no room today. People's lives, in places like this, have changed more in the last fifty years than in the five hundred before that, and a good thing too. There isn't much to regret in a way of life that condemned people to be trapped between the same hillsides and hedgerows if they didn't want to stay there, to do one kind of job because no other was accessible, to marry the girl in the next cottage because there wasn't anyone else to marry. Horizons are wider now, but through all the galloping years of change that have taken men out of the fields and on to factory assembly lines, brought primary schools and Nuffield maths and projects and creative writing, libraries and clinics, main drainage and electricity, what is surprising is the survival of people's preference for staying in the places they know.

It is an ancient place. Prehistoric peoples were using the gravel terraces of the river valleys long before the Romano-British and the Saxons began the large-scale clearances of the forest whose structure is still echoed in the placing of today's fields, roads and villages. Neolithic tombs in the Windrush Valley, Bronze Age barrows and stone circles like the Rollright Stones, Iron Age hill-forts at Idbury Camp and Tadmarton Heath, Beaker settlements between Yarnton and

Standlake. The Evenlode Valley is typical of this pattern of use, reaching away back and back into unimaginable times. North of Eynsham, it makes a wide shallow valley running between low hills. Two prehistoric roads cross here, one running north and south, and the other east and west, an old stone bridge crossing the river at a point now lost among pathless fields, but once busy with traffic. There were settlements on the hill, near Cassington, as well as down in the valley itself. This land has been in use for thousands of years, and hints of the use survive. To see the ghostly scribblings of older settlements under today's fields, look at the splendid set of aerial photographs in the Ashmolean Museum. Then, when the eye has learned what to look for, you will be able to pick out at the very least the huge ribbing of ancient field-systems that surrounds so many midland villages.

This was a part of the Saxon kingdom of Mercia, with the Thames Valley as a frontier of debatable land against Wessex. Here, the Saxons defended themselves against the Danish raids, and, farther north, held the frontiers against the Danelaw. Here they cleared the forest, yard by gruelling yard, and sank ploughshares into the heavy, unworked soil, and founded the places we live in today, for hardly a village exists that was not recorded by 1085 in the Domesday Book. This is Saxon England, preserved in its place-names, the 'tons' and 'burghs' and 'ings' and 'hams', Cassington and Hanborough and Ducklington and Eynsham, and preserved, too, here and there in something rare and more tangible – a church tower or a burial ground. But the Saxons had inherited what the Romans had left, for the Romans too were busy around here, building roads like Akeman Street that cut swaths through the landscape with a fine contempt for the dictation of hill and valley and are still here today, plunging away into the fields as a green lane or a mere thinning of the crops when the modern road parts company with them to follow a medieval wriggle or a piece of eighteenth-century turnpike. And with the roads came settlement, the construction of the villa settlements where the Romano-British lived and farmed Roman-style among the elaborate bath-houses and Mediterranean mosaics that seem so out of place in the Oxfordshire countryside. There are the sites of more than half a dozen villas in the area round Stonesfield, suggesting how extensively this piece of country must have been cleared and under plough even then. North Leigh is the best to visit, less elaborate than Chedworth over near Cirencester, but richer in that peculiar, indefinable thing called atmosphere, lying in a lush fold of the Evenlode Valley, alive with warblers in spring, empty of houses, just river and grass and wild flowers, betony and melilot and yellow archangel. I have found blue flax growing there, not a common plant in this countryside, but the Romans grew flax for making linen . . . And the Ministry of Work seems, mercifully, to have forgotten about the place and doesn't keep it too tidy – the grass grows high and there are no notices about what you may or may not do.

The Ministry of Works has no time for owls and ivy. They like their ruins smart and trim, like Hailes Abbey over in Gloucestershire, and Minster Lovell in the Windrush Valley. I see the point: you can't let the little we have left of Cistercian abbeys collapse and disappear. All the same, those immaculate paths and squares of shaven grass have little to do with the grandeur of soaring stone and the grace of gothic windows framing sky and trees. To see a real, honest, unkempt ruin you must go to Hampton Gay, where the Elizabethan manor house, destroyed by fire in 1887, stares out over lonely fields and the Banbury–Oxford railway line, saplings thrusting up between the walls and cows wandering in and out of the doorways.

There is a further reason for going to Hampton Gay. Walk across the fields from Shipton-on-Cherwell, cross the railway line, and there in the field near the isolated church are the fossilized bones of a whole village that has died and crumbled away; lumps and bumps and deep, shadowed grooves in the grass. A deserted medieval village. They exist all over England, some as clearly defined as Hampton Gay, where you can still trace the line of the village street and the position of individual houses, others almost obliterated by deep ploughing, visible only on aerial photographs or as shadowing on a field of barley when the light and the season are just right. Thanks to the work of Maurice Beresford and other historians the sites of many hundreds of deserted villages are now known, from Northumberland to Devon, silent witnesses to calamities like the Black Death, to the spread of sheep farming in the fifteenth and sixteenth centuries, and other economic pressures, or to the greed of landowners who gobbled them up to make themselves a fashionably empty park around their stately homes. The Harcourts did this at Nuneham Courtenay, and Tilgarsley near Eynsham (the exact site is in doubt) is one of the rare examples of a place where everyone died of the plague – by 1350 no one lived in a once thriving small settlement. But on the whole the reasons for the death of villages were long-term and to do with changes in farming methods, probably only dimly appreciated by the people whose lives were being disrupted. Sheep accounted for many of them as the wool-trade prospered, the old arable fields of a village vanishing to become grazing land, while other new ways of using the land meant that some places could no longer support as many people as they had done, and shrank to become a mere hamlet, or died altogether, the lands taken in by a neighbouring village. It is easy to become fascinated by lost villages, to start the search for the isolated or ruined church that suggests such a place, the patterning of ridge and furrow at a distance from other settlement, and then the give-away lumps in a field, the skin of turf over fallen stones. All you need is a pair of gum-boots, a set of 2½ inch Ordnance Survey maps, and Professor Beresford's absorbing book, *The Lost Villages of England* (or the Deserted Medieval Village Research Group's pamphlet, *The Deserted Villages of Oxfordshire*, Leicester University Press). It is tactful, though, to ask the farmer on whose land they are if he minds visitors, if there is no public footpath near.

Landscape has two faces, the open and the secret. The immediate impact of a skyline fringed with elms, stark and fragile in winter, dense and stooping in summer; skies ridged with cloud, scattered with rooks and lapwings; the blaze of a church spire among summer-heavy chestnuts; spare, stripped winter fields edged with rusty docks and skeletal heads of cow-parsley. And, behind and beyond this, the hidden clues about why, and who, and when. Why a field is shaped like this, or a green road runs between hedges and abruptly stops, and who first farmed this land, and when this village began to die, and this one to prosper. Begin to ask these questions, and you never cease. Places are never quite the same again. You see them on two different levels. You watch the shifting light that changes the mood of a piece of country from season to season and from hour to hour, from the dark greens and bright golds of high summer to the misty receding greys of winter, and at the same time you see a hedge or a twist in a road that you never noticed before, and are sent back to the maps and the books to try to find out when, and how . . .

This is a landscape of trees and ridged grey skies and the long slack lines of hills, but it is also a landscape of stone. Stone houses and stone roofs and stone walls. Whole villages and towns of it. Cotswold stone.

There is nothing like it. It has no rivals. It reflects and absorbs light in a way that perfectly matches the shifting, changing moods of this countryside: it can be grey, sharply gold, or fade to a dying cream. A wall or spire can burn apricot on a summer evening, or drain of colour to match the greys of a winter morning. It folds away into the greens and blues and fawns of hill and valley, or stands out bright and sharp to define distance and perspective. It is oolitic limestone – a legacy to us from the warm tropical seas that washed over here millions of years ago, the sedimentary rock of unthinkable aeons away, full of the fossils of brachiopods and nautili and crustacean creatures and strange black teeth of fish. It has odd names that sound more like the names of dance steps – Coral Rag and Cornbrash and Forest Marble – and it comes from

Taynton and Barrington and Windrush and Sherborne and Bladon and Charlbury and half a dozen other places, each quarry producing stone that is a little different, older or younger, give or take a million years or so, immediately distinguishable to people who know about stone. The greatest quarries of all were at Taynton, near Burford – jurassic rock from three hundred and thirty million years ago, of a fine, enduring quality, quarried for a thousand years and maybe more. The Romans knew of it, and probably used it, but its heyday came in the middle ages and later. The great wool-churches were built of Taynton stone, Burford and the others, and so were St Paul's Cathedral and Windsor Castle and Blenheim Palace. The stone for many of the Oxford colleges was carried by road to Eynsham, and from there by river to Hythe Bridge in Oxford. The quarries are abandoned now, last opened to take out the stone for the New Bodleian Library in Oxford just before the last war, but there is still stone there, great seams of it, lying undisturbed under fields and villages and roads.

And, as though the splendours of the stone were not enough, there is a further complement to it – Cotswold slate for roofs. Slate, though, is the wrong word: this is stone too, the same oolitic limestone, even richer in fossils. People who live under Stonesfield slate roofs are kept warm and dry by the remains of molluscs and corals and ferns, even the petrified bones of dinosaurs. The best slates came from Stonesfield, quarried until a hundred years ago and worked by a beautifully simple method. Stone for slating has to be split along its natural strata; at Stonesfield the quarrymen learned how to use frost to do the job for them. The stone was quarried during the autumn from shafts and galleries in the hills around the village, then it was taken to the surface and kept damp in clamps to retain the natural sap in the rock until the first hard frost came after Christmas. As soon as this happened the stone had to be uncovered and spread out for the first frost to break it up into slabs that could then be worked into slates. If the frost came at night the church bells would be rung to bring everyone out of bed to help with the business of spreading out the stone. Stonesfield slate was quarried in great quantities from the seventeenth century until the end of the nineteenth, when the quarries were closed, and will probably never be opened again, though stone for slates is still being quarried elsewhere in the Cotswolds. But we have all the Stonesfield slate we shall ever have, and what is left, enduring as it is, is shrinking into smaller and smaller slates each time a roof is repaired and the slates re-trimmed.

To see a really fine Stonesfield roof, go to the Tithe Barn at Great Coxswell. It rides the landscape like a cathedral, majestic but entirely functional, still used for the purpose for which it was built, though tractors drive in and out of the huge doors now instead of wagons and the contents are more likely to be bags of fertilizer than sacks of corn for tithes. Many of the soaring timbers are the original thirteenth-century ones, posts and trusses and tie beams, but perhaps most handsome of all is the great roof, and this was entirely stripped and re-laid in 1961. Laying a Stonesfield roof is a highly-skilled job. There are few men around capable of tackling it, which is one of the reasons why more and more old roofs are being replaced with hideous concrete tiles, about which I cannot speak calmly. But Stonesfield slates last virtually for ever; it is the rafters beneath them which must be renewed every hundred years or so. I watched a roof being re-laid recently: over 90 per cent of the slates taken down were trimmed off and put back up again, and they dated from the end of the seventeenth century at the latest. The slates are laid in courses of differing sizes, the largest at the bottom and the smallest at the top near the ridge. Each size is called by a different name, names probably as old as the process of quarrying at Stonesfield. The slater who told me the names had been taught them by an old man who learned them from his grandfather who learned them from his, which is a couple of hundred years for a start. He had, too, the grooved stick for measuring the slates which had been passed on in the same way – there is an identical one in the City and County Museum at Woodstock. I wrote the names down, because they may be forgotten one day soon, which would be sad: first, second, third, short cuttings, long cuttings, moffetty, short beck, middle beck, long beck, short batchelors, long batchelors, short nines, long nines, short wivetts, long wivetts, short elevens, long elevens, and then short and long twelves, thirteens and fourteens. Each slate is laid to overlap the one below it by two-thirds of its depth, and is chosen with care to fit close and snug to its neighbour. In re-laying old slates, some will be turned over in the search for a good fit, so that the unweathered side is uppermost – it is this random turning that gives the speckled effect which is so pleasing. They are fixed to horizontal battens laid the length of the roof – nails are used now, but the old method was with pegs made of soft-wood, which swelled to fit the round hole in the slate and rested on the batten. The pitch of Cotswold roofs is extremely steep and they are often slightly concave, not because the rafters below have sagged (though they may have) but so that the slates fit tightly to one another, like a fish's scales, and do not allow rain or wind to drive up underneath. They are immensely heavy, long-lasting, and weather-proof, and they look better than any other kind of roof. They attract moss and lichen, and so, as they weather, they turn green and gold – though, strictly speaking, the moss should not be allowed as it holds frost and can damage the slates. Once you know a little about them you appreciate the skill that goes into a well-laid roof, with dormers and swept valleys and tricky gables, and craftsmanship always has a beauty of its own. But, above all, they have the quality of looking completely natural, so that a stone-roofed house, or a whole village of stone roofs like Snowshill or Winchcombe, melts into the landscape and looks not so much as though it was built there, but simply grew.

The slater who taught me the names of the slates said to me, 'Some people, going about the place, see hills and trees and houses. I see roofs.' I knew what he meant: obsessions can blind you to everything else. Sometimes, in certain moods, I become blind to everything but churches.

When I was fourteen or so I used to accompany my grandmother and my aunt on visits to parish churches in Somerset. My grandmother and my aunt were stirred by churches: they would walk round talking knowledgeably of misericords and clerestory windows, enjoying themselves. I, on the other hand, would sit gloomily in the porch wondering how soon we could go home for tea. And then one day, in my ignorance and boredom, I began to look at the stone effigy of a crusading knight and his lady, recumbent on their tomb, and it came to me suddenly, with all the shock of a revelation, firstly that the carvings were beautiful, but secondly and perhaps even more importantly, that these had been real people who had walked in this same landscape that I walked in now. I remember feeling a leap of the imagination, being excited, and from that moment I, too, was a church addict, hunting for that shadowy link with other people, because that is what churches, above all, provide.

They are everywhere, lifting spires and towers above trees and hills, giving the perfect focal point to a valley landscape, like Burford, or rising splendidly above flat fields like Witney seen from the east. They are the centre of every village: the first and oldest building. It is hard ever to be out of sight of a church, impossible to be out of earshot. On a still day I can stand in my garden and hear the bells rung from four towers. And everywhere they are different, each one the record of a place's history and prosperity, as ancient sometimes as North Leigh with its Saxon tower, or St Michael's in Oxford, standing gaunt and amazing, one thousand years old, alongside Marks and Spencers and the daily traffic jams, or lavishly prosperous like Burford and Cirencester, stone celebrations of the wealthy wool trade. But whatever they are, light and delicate as Fairford, dourly Norman as Black Bourton, they are always, and perhaps before anything else, a roll-call of names. Names outside on tombstones, names within on brasses and memorial plaques and windows and tombs and, endlessly, on registers of births and deaths and marriages. A reminder, for ever, of who lived here, once. I look immediately for names when I go to a church. First the half-obliterated names outside in the churchyard, which will certainly be the names of people who live here still, who make up the Women's Institute and fill the pub and shriek at this moment in the school playground over the wall. And then I move on inside to the lists of rectors, starting probably with plain, unembellished Norman names, Thomas and Henry and John, and going on to the Revs, and Right Revs. and M.A.s of Victorian England. And the pious records of those who provided for the poor and also, conveniently, their own eternal souls – the perpetual prayers of 'weepers', the little stone figures that adorn so many memorials, not children but the destitute elderly, praying for a set wage. Or there are the prosperous burgesses of Burford, grown fat on Cotswold wool, salving their consciences with 'a cow for ye benefit of ye Poor', and money, 'ye interest thereof to be aply'd to ye apprenticing of poor Children', and, insuring themselves in a more practical way, endowments to keep the bridge in good repair. Burford is of all churches the one most crammed with names. Walk there alone among the memorials and it seems to shout aloud. The names clamour: people do not want to be forgotten, it is the last indignity. The one that shouts loudest, for me, is that of Anthony Sedley, who carved his name on the rim of the font on a spring night in 1649. He was a Leveller, a mutineer in Cromwell's army, imprisoned in the church with three hundred and forty others. Three of them were shot next morning in the churchyard. 'ANTHONY SEDLEY, PRISNER, 1649', he carved, with the second N back to front, because perhaps he was distracted, or hurrying, or just unsure which way was correct.

Cirencester, too, is rich in names. Names on rows of wall-plaques in lovely seventeenth- and eighteenth-century lettering, some plain records of a life, others more elaborate, like Margaret Hooper's sour warning:

Oh wreched world vayne & unsure
As I am fledd from thee
Soe mayst thou die within an houre
Then thou shalte followe me

And the contorted punning of Hodgkinson Paine, Clothier, who died at the beginning of the Civil War, in 1642:

The poore's supplie his life & calling grac't
till warres made rent & PAINE from poor displac't
But what made poore unfortunate, PAINE blest.
By warre they lost their PAINE, yet found noe rest
Hee looseing quiet by warre yet gained ease
by it PAINE's life began & paines did cease
And from ye troubles here him God did sever
by death to life, by warre to peace for ever.

Or there are exaggerated testimonies to lives which sound too virtuous to be credible, like Katherine Gregory, who is remembered in a brass at Cassington:

. . . Who Having Discharged the part of a
Dutyfull and Obedient Child,
A Tender and Deserving Wife,
an Unblameably fond Parent,
a Kind and Hospitable Neighbour,
and a Charitable Releiver of the Poor
Departed this life july 22 A.D.
1718 Aged 58

I don't believe a word of it, but the style is wonderfully elegant.

The names come first, clamouring for attention, and they must have it. When I have done with them, I start to look for the things that tell how old this church is – a rounded Norman arch with zig-zag patterning like Cassington, a door, a window, or something older yet, Saxon, a tower like North Leigh's. And then there will be all the alterations and embellishments made in later centuries, graceful medieval windows, traceries of stone and light, like Cogges (where, too, a stone frieze of bizarre and fantastic animals, fruit of riotous medieval imagery, runs round a cornice above the stolid marble busts of a seventeenth-century family, bewigged and double-chinned). Or there may be fifteenth-century fan-vaulting, springing from ribbed pillars to freeze in stone the canopy of branches splayed above a beechwood, echoing the designs of the landscape outside. Cirencester and North Leigh have such chapels, the one huge and grand, the other barely three yards long, a small miracle. Or there may be something very rare and special, like the Anglo-Saxon rood at Langford, the starkly simple Crucifixion carving on the outside wall of the church, or the windows at Fairford, and the misericords there (misericords are the carvings under the tip-up seats of choirstalls: take a torch to see the ones at Fairford properly, grotesque, explicit and funny, a dog nosing meat in a stew-pot, a woman beating her husband). Or, perhaps, best of all, it may be a church with wall-paintings.

There are so many of them – South Leigh and Widford and Combe and Beckley and Black Bourton and Hailes and South Newington . . . And there may be more yet, still hidden behind coats of plaster and whitewash. Every church was once a feast of colour and decoration, chevrons and fleur-de-lis and formal patterns in rich reds and blues covering every wall and pillar. And, above all, the great pictures of Last Judgements and Weighings of Souls and St Christophers – stories in paint, instruction for people who could not read but could understand at once the stark symbolism of devils and angels, the flames of hell and the infinite skies of heaven. At South Leigh, a mile or so away from the lorries pounding along the A40, a scarlet monster waits to devour the wicked, condemned at the Last Judgement, an uncompromising message for medieval peasants whose lives must have been bleak enough already, a prey to famine and disease. The devils with pitchforks grin down here, as they grin from the walls of so many Oxfordshire churches, released from the coating of whitewash slapped over them by later generations, disapproving the ornate mythology of medieval Christianity. Now they are back, part of the furniture of the church, along with the Victorian brass lecterns and the toppling piles of hymn books and the hassocks embroidered by members of the Women's Institute. At Widford three living kings are confronted by the skeletal shapes of three dead ones – medieval wall-paintings seldom depart from their gloomy themes of death and the hereafter. St Christopher crops up from time to time, as at Hailes in Gloucestershire where he is a huge, ghostly shape right up one wall, but he is not there in his capacity as the patron saint of travellers but because to have seen his picture protected you from sudden death – for the rest of that day. Hailes, though, has one exquisite and quite unreligious painting – a hunting scene in which lithe, greyhound-like dogs corner a hare which crouches, terrified, ears flattened, under a stylized tree. Whoever painted that had watched, outside, in green Gloucestershire, just such a scene: it is vividly, gloriously alive.

Churches, if you let them, can be a direct communication line to the past. They can provide that strange, secret charge that sets the imagination flaring – an experience you can share with no one. People have to discover it for themselves. And other places have it, too. They are powered, as it were: there is a current, live, waiting. This, for me, is what is meant by a place being haunted, and I do not believe in ghosts. Ghosts, I think, are something we need, because they have to do with our feelings about the past – with guilt and involvement and an instinct that certain things must never be forgotten. And if you need them you have to supply them yourself, from your own mind, out of what you know of a place. Know enough, feel enough, and they will come.

They are there at Edgehill, but only if you are looking for them. Go there knowing nothing of the place, and it will be only a stretch of deeply English landscape, a ridge rising sharp from soft, hilly countryside, staring away over a reach of flatter land northwards to Kineton. But go there knowing what happened on 23 October 1642, knowing something of the tormented history of seventeenth-century England, and it will be for ever peopled with the perplexed and frightened men who died there on an autumn afternoon of blue sky and sunshine. There is nothing to tell you – just an inscription on a stone by the road to Kineton which no one stops to read, and a memorial to one man in Radway church – nothing else. But it is a battlefield: twenty thousand men were here once, men and horses, and cannon and muskets and pikes. And fear and exaltation, courage and despair, screams, pain. The English Civil War began here. On these fields, among the same ditches, separated by the same slope of hill, Charles I and the Parliamentary leaders confronted each other in the bleak knowledge that argument was at an end, and violence inevitable. For the first time Englishmen killed each other over matters of principle. No wonder it is a place that cannot be forgotten. Go there in autumn, when the crops are down, as they were then, stand by the road a mile or so east of Radway, look up at the hill (wooded now, but bare then) and you are seeing the crest where the King's army waited through a long, bright autumn morning, looking down on the Parliamentary front line, drawn up just behind where you are standing. Take the Ordnance Survey map, and Brigadier Young's book on the battle, and you can work out the position of infantry and cavalry, of Prince Rupert's charge, see how the ordered, textbook formation of the morning must have become the chaos and collapse of the afternoon. It was a battle that nobody won, but at which two thousand men died. It is a silent place now, and lapwings plunge over the bright fields that are still lumpy with ridge and furrow – the same ridge and furrow of the open village fields on which the battle was fought. A silent place, secretive, and haunted. Men died here.

Otmoor is charged, too. Charged with the resentment and bitterness of the nineteenth-century villagers whose dismal lives drove them to make their own pathetic stand against the landowners who were methodically and by Act of Parliament removing the little they had – the open moor on which they grazed their geese and cattle.

> The fault is great in Man or Woman
> Who steals a goose from off the Common
> But who can plead that man's excuse
> Who steals the Common from the Goose?

The old jingle about enclosure hardly hints at the bleak suffering behind it.

But on Otmoor they fought back. A thousand strong, men, women and children, from Charlton and Oddington and Beckley and Noke and Fencot and Murcot, they tramped their way over the streaming, marshy place that is Otmoor to hack down with billhook and axe the fences that were keeping them from their traditional livelihood, the sparse grazing of the moor. They risked transportation to Australia, or even death. It was a period of unrest all over the countryside. People lived close to starvation. There were riots, rick-burning, machine-breaking. The French Revolution was barely forty years away, a spectre that haunted the English middle-classes: the rebellious labourer could expect no leniency. The Otmoor men, fifty or so of them, were arrested by red-coated militia as they smashed the hedges, were loaded into farm-carts, and driven to Oxford prison. But it was the day of St Giles' Fair. When the crowds at the fair saw the carts they fell on them and released the prisoners, the soldiers unable – or unwilling? – to do anything to prevent them. Dramatic, but not the end of the story. The Otmoor men straggled home, were re-arrested, tried and convicted. The only unexpected twist was that the savage sentences that seemed around the corner never came: they got off with six months' or a year's imprisonment. Maybe the magistrates feared reprisals more than revolution. They are long dead now, all the players in a remote, local drama that has a lot to tell about the social history of England in the nineteenth century, but Otmoor is much the same. It still streams with water – the drainage scheme that set the whole thing off never did work. I have seen minute fish swim in the ruts left by tractor tyres in high summer. Surrounded by its string of villages it lies dankly under skies that seem always a little lower and heavier than anywhere else, a place apart, different, where inadequate bus services force Otmoor people to maintain the isolation of centuries. In Charlton you can see today the nail-studded church door where the villagers stared at notices they could not understand about the Enclosure of Common Land by Act of Parliament, and the Rose and Crown Inn where they met to grumble, and plot, and finally to fight back.

And then there are other places where the charge is so weak that you can hardly pick it up. The ghosts are so far away that the effort of imagination needed to summon them is beyond most of us. The times they recall, the people, are simply too remote: we cannot know what it was like to be a person, then.

Belas Knap is one of these places – a Neolithic long barrow, near Winchcombe in Gloucestershire. You climb an amazingly steep hill, pulling yourself away from the valley up a field that seems almost vertical in places, and there at the top is this bleak little mound where four thousand years ago people chose to bury their dead. A wide and busy valley floored with orchards and neat fields and stone villages sweeps away into the blue distances of Worcestershire: then, it must have been choked with forest, impenetrable, and only these hills lifted above it, capped with green turf, accessible. They left us almost nothing, these people: bones, a few bits of broken pot, flints. They are our ancestors, but to know something of their beliefs and practices we have to look beyond the sparse suggestions of archaeological evidence and read about primitive peoples far away in New Guinea or Brazil, alive today but living at the same remote point in human development. I get restless with dry accounts of stone tools and types of pot: I want to know how people organized themselves, what they believed in, how their minds worked, and archaeology has few answers to these questions. Gloucestershire is not New Guinea, but there is a universality about primitive belief: the images of folklore echo one another round the world. Sun, water, tree, animal: birth and death. The mysterious and inexplicable natural world has been the same everywhere: people existing in the early morning of time have come up with much the same explanations, feared the same things, invested the same processes with magical significance, worshipped the same sun and placated the same dark forces.

A mile or so from Belas Knap a later people established themselves on another hill, above the village of Stanway. An Iron Age fort stood on the crest of the ridge here, protected on one side by the ditch and earthwork that can still be seen, on the other by the hillside dropping away almost sheer into the valley below. Stand up here, and you are at the junction of two wide valleys, reaching away north and east. Most of Midland England seems to lie at your feet, lush Gloucestershire and Worcestershire, with the Malverns whale-blue on the horizon and beyond them the far shadow of Wales and the Black Mountains. People came up here for the view a couple of thousand years ago, too, but they had a more urgent interest in it: up here you could see, see who might be coming to steal your cattle, burn your huts, murder your wife and children.

This is deep country. There can be nowhere more rural than this edge of Gloucestershire. You could drown here in cowparsley and meadowsweet, listening to rooks and lapwings. The jet fighters slicing through the sky from the RAF base at Kemble are unreal, a flight of fancy: such speed is not improbable, but impossible. They vanish, having reached Greenland, or the Bay of Biscay, and the cows do not even look up – they knew the things were never really there. Reality is the pattern of fields, the church spire beyond the hill, the line of elms against the sky.

One kind of reality. But at the other corner of the triangle is another – Oxford, spilling out from its tight medieval centre into its new world of factories. Oxford should have a chapter of its own. Since it cannot, and the ration of words is almost used up, it will have to be left out – almost. There is no room for colleges, churches, gardens, river, the bizarre Victorian wastes of North Oxford, for the whole odd, various, handsome, overcrowded place. I have chosen to talk about the country because this is where I am at home and where, for me, the forces that power the imagination are strongest. If I knew that I would never see Oxford again, there are only three places for which I would feel anguish – two museums, the Ashmolean and the Pitt Rivers, and the Bodleian Library.

To talk about the museums here is cheating, I suppose – they are only partly to do with England. The Pitt Rivers is to do with New Guinea and Australia and America and India and China and just about everywhere else. One day, when someone finds a spare million pounds or so, the Pitt Rivers Museum will be moved into a splendid new building and the stone axes and the totems and the grass skirts and the painted masks will be tastefully displayed in well-lit cases against careful backgrounds and I, for one, will be very sad. To go there now, through the Victorian station architecture of the Natural History Museum, is like finding yourself suddenly in someone's attic. A huge, three-storey attic in which the most astonishing, sobering demonstration of how primitive people think and behave is crammed and stacked and piled into cases and cupboards. It is the finest ethnological collection in the world: here, translated into things, into objects jumbled together behind glass, is the furniture of the savage mind – the beliefs and taboos and the superstitious magic, along with all the mundane business of living, the fish-hooks and the keys and the paraphernalia for making fire. It is a place for wet winter afternoons, for forgetting the time and straining your eyes peering at dim, hand-written labels that talk about expeditions to the Amazon in 1911. There are shrunken heads, skulls, bones, and every known implement people have ever used for killing each other. And then there are musical instruments and mysterious, unforgettable masks, yard upon yard of shell necklaces, and tiny, beautiful carvings. You come away bewildered – amazed at what it is like to be a human being.

The Ashmolean, on the other hand, is not for wet afternoons but for ten minutes whenever you feel like it, as often as possible, to visit a special favourite – the Chinese plate with the fighting dragons, or the tranquil Buddhas, or the Corot landscapes, or the German enamel dish that has a light like cold blue flame. If you have to go there with someone else, say goodbye to them firmly at the entrance and meet later: you will not want to be distracted and it is always more satisfying to make your own discoveries. When I was a child, I was towed round museums by well-meaning people, told what was admirable and what was not – I have yawned from one end of the National Gallery to the other. Years later, alone, I learned how to look at things for myself, and I am still learning. I have never cared for glass cases full of china and porcelain – I used to think them boring. The Ashmolean has taught me otherwise. They have a mysterious genius there, somewhere behind the scenes, who knows how to take a bowl and a plate and a cup, Ming and Sung and T'ang, and put them on just the right kind of material, with the light arranged just so. You see the things with new eyes, and with delight.

And then there is the Bodleian. Sometimes American tourists will stop you and say in bewilderment, 'Where is the University?' They may well ask – it is almost a metaphysical concept, all round them, and yet nowhere in particular. The Bodleian is the same. It is the Radcliffe Camera and the New Bodleian and Rhodes House and the Taylorian Institute and a good deal of it lies mysteriously somewhere underground. Its central core, I suppose, is the catalogue room. Here, in hundreds of immense volumes so heavy that you need two hands to lift them, are the titles of the million odd books the Bodleian owns. Think of a book, any book, look up its shelf mark, fill in a pink form, post the form into a little box, wait, and lo! the book will arrive. It is a process that never ceases to astonish: infinitely benevolent, it seems, like the enactment of a wish. Here you are, standing in this big high room that has a peculiar smell of its own (not of books, but some eccentric variety of furniture polish favoured by the Curators) and there, out of sight but to be conjured up with a few words on a piece of paper, is everything that has ever been written. All the knowledge in the world, all the literature, all the thought, all the achievement. It is enough to send you reeling out into Radcliffe Square again.

The Bodleian, like the British Museum, is a copyright library. That is to say that every publisher is obliged to send it a copy of every book they publish. And then, of course, it takes in periodicals and magazines and newspapers. You could sit under the ornate fifteenth-century ceiling of Duke Humphrey's Library and read back numbers of *Beano*, if you felt so inclined. It keeps everything, a squirrel-hoard: everything must be available – sometime, one day, someone may need it. There are two First Folio Shakespeares here, and the Gutenberg Bible; medieval Books of Hours – the pages fringed with meticulous, glowing illumination; a manuscript of the Canterbury Tales; first editions – Keats, Chaucer, *Gulliver's Travels*; a draft of the 'Ode to the West Wind'. . . And the manuscript of *The Wind in the Willows*. And a first edition of *Bradshaw's Railway Timetable*. And then there are boxes upon boxes of letters, and pamphlets, and title deeds to houses, and inventories, and menus, and boxes whose contents are so miscellaneous that nobody knows what is inside them until someone, looking for something else, orders them up and finds out. It is like a vast stomach, digesting everything, with only the catalogue as a tenuous link with what may be inside. If a book is put back in the wrong place it is as irretrievably lost, almost, as if it were stolen: it might be fifty years before the mistake is detected.

We have come full circle, from a place where people first began to snatch a living in these parts, to one of the greatest libraries in the world, whose business it is to preserve the record of everything they have done since. All within twenty miles or so. It's an odd place, this middle part of England: as ancient as its own hills, as new as its factories and air-bases – busy, compact, various. To live here, to put down roots, is to find a new meaning in the permanence of place: you live with tree and hill and river, and you live too with the people who came before, whose landscape, also, it is. A haunted place.

I WAS BORN IN THE MIDLANDS

by Helen Cresswell

Who am I to say that I wish I had been born elsewhere? Who *would* I have been, had I not been born in Kirkby-in-Ashfield, bred in a Nottingham suburb, and am even now living in a north Nottinghamshire village? Certainly not the 'I' who am writing this now. Because what we are is very largely where we are, of that I am certain. The poet says, 'Stone walls do not a prison make', but we must allow for his licence. Four stone walls and a high barred window would seem to me to be very much like a prison. And although I think my imagination is as powerful as most, some unretractable, instinctive part of me cannot agree that one place is as good as another, that we must rise above our surroundings.

I, for one, do not want to rise above my surroundings. It is too much hard work. I would wish my surroundings to be such that I had no wish to escape them, to invent imaginary landscapes of my own. Meanwhile, I live in Nottinghamshire, with my eyes wide open, looking always with hope for something to admire, something to love, even.

My earliest memory of Nottinghamshire is of a coal tip. I used to lie in my grandmother's high feather bed, the clock ticking loudly by my ear, and watch the little trucks run steeply up against the skyline. And I would think how brave and busy they looked, ceaselessly running up and down at six o'clock in the morning – all by themselves, it seemed, for there was no sign of human life. I thought the tips were black, conical mountains, a special landscape, and it never occurred to me to think them ugly. Nor do I now. There is a strange beauty in the tower and wheels of a pit-head against the sky. After all, it is rooted, deeply rooted, into the earth, and so as much a part of it as a tree. And at night, when the floodlights make a circle of misty light that blots out moon and stars and draws a special night world of its own out of the darkness, there is a glamour and mystery about it that no string of sodium town lights could ever have.

I remember all kinds of things about Kirkby-in-Ashfield, which typically was half rural, half industrial, a hybrid. D. H. Lawrence describes just such a place in *Lady Chatterley's Lover*:

'Wragby stood on an eminence in a rather fine old park of oak trees, but alas, one could see in the near distance the chimney of Tevershall pit, with its clouds of steam and smoke, and on the damp, hazy distance of the hill the raw struggle of Tevershall village, a village which began almost at the park gates, and trailed in utter hopeless ugliness for a long and gruesome mile: houses, rows of wretched, small, begrimed brick houses, with black slate roofs for lids, sharp angles and wilful, blank dreariness.'

But beyond the pit and the rows of narrow, terraced houses,

were always the fields, there was always a glimpse of green somewhere behind the smoky bricks. I remember evening, dew-smelling walks down the cow pastures. There we leapt with squeals of fear and daring over the large cow-pats, always keeping a wary eye over the shoulder at the cows themselves. The long shadows made the fields seem hummocky and mysterious, our eyes were flooded with the level sun.

In those days miners would walk about the streets still wearing their boots and gear, and with hands and faces ditched black. Why did miners have such white, red-rimmed eyes, I wondered, and why such flashing teeth and unnaturally red lips? My grandfather on my father's side was a miner, and so had my father himself been, in the early days, and knowing this gave him a special status in my eyes, made a hero out of him.

A month or so ago I went down a mine in the village next to the one where we now live. (I see its lights from my bedroom window, I hear its lonely siren in the night.) And I saw then that my early instinct had been a true one, that there *is* a kind of heroism in the life of a miner, that to hew roads out of rock and coal half a mile below ground is not the work of an ordinary man. The very air he breathes is different. I smelled it first in the great, descending cage, that dry, coal-smelling air, and once down there I met the rushing warm winds that funnel through the corridors, mile upon mile, like the winds in a tube station.

The miner crouches to work on the coal face itself, his vision limited to the beam of light from his own helmet lamp, focused always on the step ahead, the job in hand, the danger. Because danger there is. Only a major mining disaster reaches the national headlines. But in the local press, week by week, you may read of the single miner who has died down there. At Stavely Church, in Derbyshire, there is a lamp that burns ceaselessly as a tribute to the men who risk their lives daily, and to those who have died down there in the dark.

It is a miner's lamp burning forever
Near a piece of coal in Stavely Church.

My earliest memories are all of black-faced miners, tips, tiny, soap-smelling sculleries and warm, rough people. But these are the memories of visits. In West Bridgford, where I lived from early childhood to adulthood, our house was neat and semi-detached and on a tree-lined street with slab pavements. All the time I lived there I was homesick. There are suburbs like this around every large town in England, where people wall themselves in and grow lilac bushes and weeping willows.

I wish I could tell you how the people are, apart from the miners and those who work on the land. In one sense they are like people anywhere and everywhere. But there is the subtle, indefinable difference that comes of the very fact of their living in Nottinghamshire, whether as natives or by choice. And then there are so many different kinds of place and landscape.

West Bridgford, for instance, was known when I was a child as 'bread and lard island'. What it meant was that the people who lived there had paid their last farthings for the privilege of living in its respectable, tree-lined streets, with front gardens neatly mown and dug. It meant that the mock Tudor semi-detacheds and the wrought-iron gates were only a façade, behind which people grubbed and cheese-pared, paying the price of a minor gentility. These were not so much homes as fortresses, fiercely held after first being hard won. The people who lived there were nearly all first generation middle class, their roots in slum and terrace. Their uncertainty bred an iron conventionality, a rigid framework of rules to be kept – always clean socks and shiny shoes for the children, and no swearing, and keep the front room tidy in case of visitors, and dry worn-out clothing on a horse by the fire, instead of hanging it out on the line for the neighbours to see and talk about.

These suburbs were the landscape of my childhood, and I

can even think with nostalgia of the whirr of lawn mowers on summer evenings, the slabbed pavements ready-made for hopscotch, the rides on the tops of buses with views into bedrooms, the orderly, unquestioning conformity with your neighbours. In the suburbs you can be safe as houses if only you do as the others do. And there is no harm in a child feeling as safe as houses. There will be time later to rebel, to begin thinking, to find chinks in the walls.

I do not like large cities. Their sheer size weighs on me, threatens to blot me out. In any case, I am irretrievably committed to a passion for the countryside. And this passion, I can only think, is partly instinctive and partly a result of my early reading – Keats, Wordsworth, Hardy, the Brontës. I have a blind spot where cities are concerned, and am unfair to them because I do not understand them. Cities are places of commerce, and I do not understand that, either.

As a child I would walk in Nottingham with my mother through the crowds and marvel at the size of it all, and be half fearful because in a single afternoon's shopping I could look into a thousand strange faces and see not a sign of recognition or awareness in them. Now I have learned, slowly and painfully, not to *look* at people's faces as I hurry through the city on an inescapable errand. Through sheer self-defence I have learned the trick of 'shutting off' that curious, searching part of me that wants instinctively to relate to everyone and everything it sees. But this trick seems to me to be not a development, but a regression. I have given up trying to relate to a city. The bombardment of my senses is too much for me.

And so I can say hardly anything at all about the county towns of Nottingham and Derby that could not as easily be found in a guide book. Nottingham itself is proud and wealthy, the Queen of the Midlands. It is a fine city, with conscious civic pride, a long history, and its weather eye on the gold it harvests from its many industries – lace, coal, leather, bicycles, cigarettes, drugs. It is all the time severing the roots that lie in the past. Year by year the old landmarks disappear making room for developments of multi-storey office blocks and flats. Sometimes the changes are for the better. Slum clearance is making way for houses better to look at and better to live in. But sometimes the motives for destruction seem less commendable, and all the little alleys and by-ways known as the Lace Market that centre round the ancient church of St Mary are disappearing into the hungry jaws of the bulldozer.

But then I am incurably prejudiced in favour of beauty against progress, wherever they come into conflict (which is everywhere and all the time). It always seems to me that with a little more patience, we could have both – beauty and progress. I echo the views of John Ruskin, who, when the five-arched railway bridge was built over the beautiful River Wye near Longstone Edge in Derbyshire, wrote:

'You might have seen the gods there morning and evening, walking in fair procession on the lawns, and to and fro among the pinnacles of its crags, but the valley is gone, and the gods with it. And now every fool in Buxton can be in Bakewell in half an hour, and every fool in Bakewell at Buxton.'

I am aware of the flaws in such an attitude, but do not apologize for it. It provides a necessary balance.

Under the city of Nottingham itself is a catacomb of caves. I never walk from the great slab square, up Friar Lane and Maid Marion Way, without thinking of them there under my feet. I find it oddly satisfying to think that these towering new structures are built on a rock, but on a sandstone rock, riddled with gigantic holes. I have been down there, through a yawning entrance in somebody's back garden, behind the laurels. And to advance even fifty yards into the dark, damp and mineral-smelling darkness was to feel excited, and afraid. To be in the dark and underground is to be out of time and almost out of place.

Robin Hood lurked once in these caves. He came to bait the Sheriff of Nottingham, and statues of himself and his Merrie Men line the verge beneath the castle walls to prove it.

The castle itself has a history dating back to Norman times, when William Peverel built it on the rock that dominates the city. In the fourteenth century Edward III secretly entered the castle by the passage through the rock known as Mortimer's Hole, which visitors can still go down today. It was from here that Richard set out for Bosworth Field, and here that Charles Stuart raised his standard at Standard Hill. Colonel Hutchinson held the castle for Parliament during the Civil War, and the story of his heroism can be read in Lucy Hutchinson's memoirs of her husband's life. But when the war was over the castle was almost demolished, and though the first Duke of Newcastle rebuilt parts, it was again attacked and fired by a mob of stockingers during the industrial revolution, and was a blackened and roofless shell for over forty years. Now rebuilt and still magnificent, it is an art gallery and museum.

One of Nottingham's oldest traditions is the great Goose Fair, held during the first week of October every year. It has long since ceased to be a fair for hiring, or for the buying and selling of livestock. Now it is a great, glorious, incomparable fun fair, held on the steeply sloping sweep of green about a mile north of the city centre known as The Forest. To an outsider, it might seem like any other fun fair, only bigger.

To a native of Nottingham, who as a child has been taken there and seen for the first time from the top of The Forest the sudden huge blaze of light and colour lying below in the dusk of an October evening, it is a place of magic. People in these parts, as autumn draws on, sniff at the air and say 'Goose Fair weather!' and are speaking, without knowing it, out of the childhood memory, fixed for ever now, of the sheer smell of excitement, like that of a real Christmas tree or of a burnt-out firework. We go as adults to indulge our nostalgia, in the vain hope of recapturing the smell and sound and feel of those early visits, when a monkey on a stick or a goldfish in a bowl were trophies beyond price, the gifts of wizards. You would put them by your bedside that night and hardly expect them still to be there in the morning.

I think that a native of Nottingham returning on a sentimental visit would make for the Trent Embankment between Trent Bridge and the Wilford Toll Bridge. There can hardly be a Nottinghamian alive who has not found himself down there *some* weekend in his life. It is a fine, curving sweep of embankment, a promenade, and the Trent is lined on the city side by seven or eight deep steps, so that you can walk along them for a mile or more, stepping up or down to avoid the anglers and boys with jampots on the end of string, and families with bags of crusts for the swans. From Trent Bridge in the summer you can take a pleasure trip to Colwick (home of the cheeses) or Wilford, and there are rowing boats for hire. There is a holiday spirit on a fine weekend down the Embankment – all the children seem to be licking ices.

There are plenty of wide green spaces in Nottingham. The University, endowed by Jesse Boot, must be one of the most splendid in the country, set as it is in sweeping acres of grounds, with lake, and bordered by masses of rhododendrons along the fine, wide University Boulevard. Then there is Wollaton Park, of nearly 800 acres, still grazed by deer. Its centre is Wollaton Hall, now a natural history museum, built originally during the reign of Elizabeth I.

Nottingham claims Robin Hood as its hero, but his real home was the greenwood, in Sherwood Forest, and the great Major Oak is still there, at Edwinstowe, only a few miles from where we now live. Its massive boughs are propped and chained, it is like a captive, wounded beast, splinted and bound. But it *is* alive, and a marvel, carrying the centuries on its back. When I walk in the forest early in the morning when it is deserted, and hear the falling wail of the pit sirens, it is easy enough to hear instead Robin's bugle sounding thinly through the trees. Sherwood is beautiful still, especially in the autumn when the silver birches rise from a sea of bracken and fern lit auburn in the low sunlight. Here and there are trees so old that they stand blackened and bitten as though the life in them were so weak that they are inert as rocks.

For me, this is the best part of Nottinghamshire, the north-eastern stretch that is really a great tract of wooded parkland, the thousands of acres of the Dukeries. Here are the great houses of Thoresby, Clumber and Welbeck, and the old Rufford estate with its great lake. As you drive north you pass the stone lodges and high, wrought-iron gates and noble avenues of trees. Deer still graze in the parks, and the whole region is hunting and shooting country still, though bows and arrows have long been replaced by guns. I dare not go out walking in the winter in a fur hat. They shoot at anything that is furry and moves, in these parts. In the graveyard at Eakring, where we live, once part of the Rufford estate, is the headstone of a gamekeeper with this inscription:

> Here lies Edward Cartwright Senior Late Keeper to His Grace the Duke of Kingston 55 Years. He died February 13 1773 aged 80 Years 10 Months and Three Weeks.
>
> My Gun discharged my ball is gone
> My Powder spent my work is done.
> Those panting Deer I Have left behind
> May now have time to gain their wind
> Who I have ofttimes chased them O're
> The Verdant Plains, but now no more.

This church has a strong link with Eyam, in Derbyshire, where at the time of the plague, in September 1665 a box of tailor's cloth and some old clothes came from London to a cottage by the church, and with it death for 259 out of 350 villagers. Here the rector, William Mompesson and his wife stayed to minister to the sick, and voluntarily isolated the village from the outside world. They arranged for food and other necessities to be put at certain fixed places, the money left for payment being carefully washed. One of these places,

Mompesson's Well, is still there, covered by a block of stone, just north of the village.

It was three years after the plague that Mompesson came to Eakring. Yet the villagers were still so afraid that they would not let him come to the church, and he had to live for a time in a hut in Rufford Park. Each day a villager would bring him food, leaving it at a safe distance. And just above Eakring, in a lonely spot by a hedge in a field, there is a simple memorial to this brave man. The spot is known as Pulpit Ash, because it was here, out in the open, that Mompesson would preach to his cowardly flock. An Ash tree grows there still, but it is not the original one. Mompesson stayed in Eakring as rector for thirty-eight years and died in 1708.

Now, three hundred years after the plague, a coach party sets out from Eakring to Eyam on Feast Day, the last Sunday in August, and the two villages jointly commemorate the story. They tread the way in procession from the church to yet another open-air pulpit from which Mompesson preached, an arched rock known as Cucklet Delf.

History takes longer to die in the countryside than it does in towns. Country families have often lived in the same parts for generations, and stories passed on by word of mouth are always longer remembered than those read in books. And even the obscure can live on in a village, the 'unsung dead' that Gray writes of in his Elegy.

We have heard, little by little, the stories of those who lived before us in our two-hundred-year-old farmhouse – of the butcher who lived here, then left and within a month had hanged himself at Mansfield. And of old Aunt Polly, who on her death bed shammed sleep when the rector came to call, and the minute he had left sat bolt upright and abused him roundly. For years after her death little bags of sovereigns were found here and there through the house, hoarded squirrel-like. On the south side of the house is a great pear tree, its boughs trained along the wall (and keeping it up, most likely), and its pears weigh little short of a pound each. Old

Aunt Polly would count her pears year by year, and if one was missing, then all hell would break loose. We often think that if our house is haunted, we shall find out in the autumn, at pear time, when Polly rises to confront us with pointing finger of accusation.

I often wander through the rambling, overgrown graveyard, parting the long grasses to read the inscription of the Hannahs, the Polly Anns and the Samuels late of this parish. And I cannot imagine that these people were very different from those who still live and work in Eakring. They are forthright, drily humorous and above all, honest. Only last week a neighbour told me of a conversation that had taken place at her weekly sewing class at nearby Maplebeck. And this story seems to me to epitomize the character of these north Nottinghamshire people.

'There's this woman been coming to our class for years. May Toole, she's called, and forty-five, I s'pose. Face always long as a fiddle but she's that *funny*, and never moves her face an inch while she's talking, but rest of us, we're in *stitches*. And last year she had one of these hysterectomies. And she keeps going on about she's lost weight, and always asking us do she look well. And last week she says to me, "Do I look well to you, Mary?" and I says, "Course you do, silly so-and-so. You pack up smoking them cigarettes and get some food down you, and you'll be right as rain." Then she starts on about her lying-in gown – not that we ain't heard about *that* afore, a dozen times. Wonder is she need to *go* to sewing class, if you was to believe how wonderful this here gown is. Started it when she was twenty-one, and been kept in chest ever since, waiting while it's needed. Lovely job she made of it, from what she says – beautiful. We ain't none of us seen it, but she put some work in – tucks and flounces and the Lord knows. Well anyway, last week, she said to Albert (that's her husband), "Albert, if I was to *go* – you know, if I *was* to go, should you put up a stone for me, like? Headstone?"

"Go?" says Albert. "You?"

"If I *was* to," says May. "Should you?"

"Aye, well . . . I s'pose so," says Albert. "Aye, I should think I should."

"Well listen, Albert," says May, "I've been having a look into them, and pricing 'em, them headstones. And I reckon to get one worth putting up, you'd be paying out all of seventy-five pound."

"Aye, well," says Albert. "It's a lot o' money. But we shall have to see about that, when we come to it."

"But Albert," says May, "I've been thinking on it, and it do seem a dreadful lot o' money. And Albert . . . 'stead of stone, could I have money *now*, d'ye think, for there's something I'm wanting awful bad!"'

And there we have it.

Between Eakring and Newark, we drive past villages with names like Maplebeck and Winkburn, still with populations of only a hundred or two, and not a house built for over a century. If you walk there, particularly on one of those hot summer days that are peculiarly deep and still and filled with the drone of insects, you can actually feel time come to a standstill. You can stand in the knee-deep grass of the graveyard and smell the hot nettles and the dry yews and be in a kind of no man's land, out of time. You can come home and see cars and the television and all the other paraphernalia of twentieth-century life with a shock, a definite startled awareness that you *are* anchored in time, after all, like it or not. Though I am not a great believer in time myself. There are some moments you could weigh against a whole century.

Only five miles away is the little cathedral town of Southwell. Southwell Minster is perhaps the least-known cathedral in England, and one of the most beautiful, with its twin spires and Norman arches and spacious green setting. It has a stone screen six hundred years old, and to stand and stare at it is to see not only a miraculous piece of craftsmanship, but a work of philosophy, where virtues and vices stand personified, and every carved head, every detail, tells a story. Best of all is the chapter house, built like that of York in octagonal shape and with thirty-six seats each with a triangular stone canopy. The carving here is a work of genius – detailed, lively, humane, and always true to nature. Every leaf has a stem, acorns are shown tumbling to be eaten by the carved swine below, and two dogs run to earth a hare among the ivy that gamekeepers say the hare always seeks when it is about to die.

Southwell has the slow-moving, assured pace of any other cathedral town. In its centre are streets of fine Georgian houses set in spacious grounds. The pavements are so narrow that there are constant side-steppings, and the constant decision as to whether a mother and pram takes precedence over an elderly deacon's widow, or vice versa. The Saracen's Head, opposite the Cathedral, is a coaching inn with a courtyard entered by a stone archway. It was here that Charles Stuart stayed for a few hours before giving himself up at nearby Kelham to a captivity that ended on the scaffold.

As you approach Newark from the north the sign says, 'Welcome to the ancient and historic town of Newark upon Trent', and you are immediately made aware of history in the romantic ruins of the castle just across the river. It was here that King John died in 1216, and it was made a ruin during the Civil War when it remained loyal to King Charles and withstood three sieges.

For thirty years of my life I lived within twenty miles of Newark and had never visited it – only passed through. Everyone who lives in the Midlands has passed through Newark at one time or another, on the way to the east coast, to Skegness, Mablethorpe or Sutton-on-Sea. But Newark is not a town to be by-passed, it is a place to linger in and explore.

Twice-weekly a market is held in the cobbled square – a square you will never see if you merely pass through. It is dominated by the magnificent tower and spire of the old parish church of St Mary, and surrounded on all sides by Tudor buildings and old inns. At the Saracen's Head Charles Stuart slept, at the Clinton Arms Byron stayed to see his first volume of poems through the press, and in 1868 George Eliot stayed at the old Ram Inn by the castle.

I discovered only recently that Kate Greenaway, famous as an illustrator of children's books, would often visit Newark market as a child. She stayed for long periods of her childhood with her great-aunt, Mrs Wise, at the little village of Rolleston about eight miles from where I live. I went to look at it, and found the old part of the village much as it must have been then, but now the landscape is irrevocably ruined by the enormous power station at nearby Staythorpe. Kate spent many of her happiest days here, both with her aunt and with an old servant, Mary Chappel, who lived in a little red-brick cottage on the road towards Fiskerton. And from there they would set off for Newark market in her aunt Aldridge's high dog cart, and have their lunch there at one of the inns among the farmers and their wives – just as our family often does today. And then she would wander among the noisy stalls and wonder why people bought groceries when they could afford peppermints (as doubtless my own eight year-old daughter does now).

Newark is certainly most worth seeing on Thursdays and Saturdays when the country people come in for the market and the square is closed to traffic. A real market, this, with flowers and fruit and vegetables straight from the fields – with the dew still on them, practically. Newark is a marvellous place for food, every other shop seems to be a pastry cook or a pork butcher, and the shoppers themselves have the glossy, amiable look of those who work in the open and have a healthy liking for their stomachs. They are people who look much the same now as they would have done twenty or thirty years ago, dressed in honest-to-goodness clothes, the women in felt hats and stout shoes and hardly a dollyrocker in sight.

In contrast, the crowds in Mansfield, only twenty miles to the west, seem pale and ill-favoured, rude and shoving. If you take a pram to Mansfield on a market day it is at the risk of having it turned over, baby and all. We never go to Mansfield if we can avoid it. There are good things here and there – the indoor market, for instance, cool and echoing and richly stocked as any you might find in Brittany. And the best pork sausages in the county are to be bought in Mansfield, so they say. But for the most part it is mean and ill-favoured – an ugly town. The midlands are full of towns and villages like this, and they always arouse in me a kind of desperation mixed with sorrow.

D. H. Lawrence was born and lived in such a place, Eastwood, near the Nottinghamshire and Derbyshire border. *Sons and Lovers* is steeped in the very essence of this locality. And this writer had the same ambivalent attitude towards his birthplace as I myself admit to. The urban and industrial landscape (and much of the life lived there) is, he says, 'ugly, ugly, ugly'. But the countryside is beautiful, strong, as if it had a backbone, was made of sterner stuff than much of the southern pastoral scene. Walking in north Nottinghamshire you do not meet people who look like dreaming poets, or sentimentalists, but men in cloth caps exercising whippets, gamekeepers, and men who are simply striding out to save their bus fare, as their fathers did before them.

Nonetheless, a dreaming poet did once walk the countryside around Mansfield. Only a few miles away is Newstead Abbey, where Lord Byron lived. Henry II built this monastery for Black Canons as part of a penance for the murder of Becket, and it was only when the monks were scattered at the time of the Reformation that the Abbey came into the hands of Sir John Byron of Colwick. By the time the poet inherited it, it had fallen into such decay that he wrote of it:

'Through thy battlements, Newstead, the hollow winds
  whistle;
  Thou, the hall of my fathers, art gone to decay:
In thy once smiling garden the hemlock and thistle
  Have choked up the rose which late bloomed in thy way.'

Byron came to live there after leaving Cambridge, but in the end, despite his love for the place, became so heavily in debt that he was forced to sell it. Now the historic part of the Abbey is open to the public, and one can see all the Byron relics, with his bedroom and dressing-room as he left them, the original paper still on the walls. In the grounds are a beautiful natural lake and also the rectangular Eagle Pond, into which the fleeing monks threw their treasures, including a brass eagle lectern. This is now in Southwell Minster, but later the old deeds of the Abbey were found concealed in the pedestal, and these are now divided between Newstead and the British Museum. Close by the Eagle Pond is the famous monument raised by the poet to his dog Boatswain, who had, so he says, 'beauty without vanity, strength without insolence, courage without ferocity, and all the virtues of man without his vices'.

My part of the Midlands, oddly, appeals to me more now than it did as a child. I think that since I have been able to rove the counties at will by car and on foot, I have the feel of them better. My daily landscape as a child was that of any other suburban child in any industrial provincial city. From time to time, on occasional picnics and day outings, I would see glimpses of the countryside, and especially the Derbyshire landscape (because the grass on the other side of a county boundary is always greener to a picknicker).

But always when we went to Derbyshire we seemed to end up at Matlock, and always for some reason on a grey day that ended in rain. And the grey stone town overshadowed by towering crags on either hand, always gave me a feeling of fear and foreboding. Even now, as an adult, Matlock depresses me. And the road from Nottingham to Derby that we travelled in those days was through a dreary conurbation of little mining towns and villages, lined by smoky red-brick terraces and villas, by ugliness.

But now I can see in my mind's eye the sweep of the two counties, can savour the essence of them, from the gently rolling Vale of Belvoir in south Nottinghamshire to the stark grandeur of the Derbyshire Peak District. And if I do not wholeheartedly love the county of my birth (or if, rather, I love the parts of it rather than the whole), and if my feelings are lukewarm, then the reason, I suspect, lies within myself. It lies within my temperament, or in some early, flawed encounters with the environment that have never been wholly overcome.

In Derbyshire is some of the most beautiful scenery in England, including the greater part of the Peak District National Park. The River Dove, and its tributary, the Manifold, are what I call 'secret' rivers – you have to look for them. If it were possible, it would be best of all to come upon them by chance. If you 'discovered' the Dove or the Manifold for yourself, you would be under its spell for life. And even at weekends, when people flock by the thousand to Dovedale near Thorpe Cloud, it is possible to walk just a little farther than the many, to become one of the few who really follow the pull of the valley, as if drawn by an invisible thread.

Izaak Walton, author of *The Compleat Angler*, was a friend of Charles Cotton of nearby Beresford Hall, and a Fishing Temple stands in Beresford Dale with their monograms carved over the door. And I think that even I could become a fisherman (or at least pretend to be one) for the sake of days spent in these beautiful valleys where the light filters greenish gold down through the woods on either hand.

There are spas and market towns and villages in Derbyshire that all have a strange sameness for me. Perhaps it is because their names seem so alike – Buxton, Bakewell, Ashbourne, Bolsover, Ashford, Ashover – but more, I think, because there *is* an essential sameness. It is not just the grey Derbyshire stone (and the whole county is mapped out with grey stone walling), the style of architecture, the steep streets. It is an atmosphere almost indefinable. These places always seem to be not quite on the map. I find myself, for instance, noticing television aerials and thinking suddenly, with something like shock, 'The people who live here have television – they watch the very same programmes as I!'

I find that I cannot imagine them reading the same newspaper nor going to the same place for their holiday – nor indeed being anywhere out of their own context. And now that I think about it, I cannot recall that I have ever met a single person who came from Derbyshire. Perhaps people do not come from Derbyshire. They stay there, held by the mesmeric spell that I myself have felt even on day visits, a spell that I half fear.

There are many old customs preserved in Derbyshire. They draw the curious tourists, but are nonetheless private, *theirs*, the Derbyshire men's, and they mean something. You cannot visit a village at well-dressing time without being aware that gods are being placated, rites observed with due solemnity. These are no empty echoes of dead beliefs.

There are well dressings at Wirksworth, Youlgreave, Bonsall, Eyam and many more. But the loveliest of all is at the beautiful village of Tissington, on Holy Thursday. The Tissington Wells saved its inhabitants at the time of the Black Death, and then again from drought in the seventeenth century. There are five of them – the Hands Well, the Hall Well, the Town Well, the Yew Tree Well and the Coffin Well (a trough-shaped well in a cottage garden).

The local people gather moss and flowers and leaves, and press them into salted clay to form living pictures and designs. They are intricate as stained-glass windows, some telling a parable, others illustrating a text. They glow and shine and are a marvel of living folk art. On Ascension Day, when the wells are literally in full flower, there is first a service in the tiny church and then a procession visits every well in turn. A hymn or psalm is sung at every halt, a prayer offered, and the water blessed by the vicar. The people of Derbyshire love their wells and honour them as the life-giving sources that they are.

At beautiful Ashford in the Water the old custom of ringing the curfew each day is still observed, and the Pancake Bell is rung on Shrove Tuesday. Here in the church still hang five paper garlands, the 'Maidens' Garlands'. The custom was to carry these in the funeral processions of village maidens, and leave them in the church. Garlands of this kind are also to be found at Matlock and Turlsley. Even at Ashover, with its quarries and railways, there is history in the church. One of the bells in the tower bears the proud boast that it 'rang the downfall of Bonaparte and broke April 1814'. The stout ringers of Derbyshire rang their bells till they cracked! In the register of this same church is the death of one Dorothy Matley, whose story is told as a solemn parable of sudden judgement in John Bunyan's *Life and Death of Mrs. Badman*:

'Take that dreadful story of Dorothy Matley of Ashover, a liar and thief that washed the rubbish that came from the lead mines. Her usual way of asserting things was with imprecations such as "I would I might sink into the earth!"

On 23 April she was washing on a hill and was there taxed by a lad for taking twopence out of his pocket. She denied it, wishing the ground might swallow her if she had them. Now a man of good report came by and saw her with her tub and sieve twisting round and sinking into the ground, and a great stone fell on her head, the earth fell in on her, and she was afterwards found four yards within the ground, the boy's twopence in her pocket.'

In Derbyshire, that is a twopennyworth that might well have happened – might almost happen still.

Derbyshire and Nottinghamshire meet at the mining village of Creswell where the ancient Creswell Crags have one foot in either county. Here are the caves where treasures made by Britain's earliest men have been found – caves with names like Robin Hood's Cave, Church Hole, Mother Grundy's Parlour and the Pin Hole.

Sir William Boyd Dawkins, digging there over seventy years ago, found the earliest example of pictorial art known in Britain – a piece of smooth bone on which had been scratched the head and shoulders of a horse. Layer by layer the cave floors were excavated, and remains were found, incredibly, of the hippopotamus, rhinoceros and hyena – all animals that need a much warmer climate than ours. These were the survivors of the Pliocene into the early Pleistocene Age, and the men who made the quartzite implements also found there, must have eaten the flesh of these beasts, for signs of fire were found in the bones.

Later, during excavations of the Pin Hole Cave, evidence was found that at least two glacial periods had passed over Creswell Crags. And most mysterious, the egg shell, perfectly preserved, of a kind of goose was found, with a narrow hole through which the cave man had sucked its contents. Other treasures found were engravings on bone and ivory, and flint tools used over twenty thousand years B.C.

The historical houses of Derbyshire are well known – Chatsworth, Haddon, Hardwick, Melbourne, Sudbury. My own favourite is Haddon Hall – romantic and picturesque, the very ideal of medievalism. The oldest part is the chapel with its Norman font, medieval glass windows and wall paintings. But Haddon's charm for me lies in its domesticity, its air of having been intimately lived in, despite its size and grandeur. It is a place of nooks and corners, little courtyards and corners to be turned, as well as sweeping proportions – the Long Gallery, for instance, measures 110 feet in length. I far prefer it to Hardwick Hall, chilling in its magnificence and symmetry, and with its 290-feet frontage.

When I was a child there was a rhyme we used to chant:

'Derby born and Derby bred
Strong in the arm and weak in the head.'

And while this is not literally true, it does seem that Derbyshire's great men have tended to have a practical rather than an artistic bent. It is as if the sheer sweep and power of the landscape forced its natives into turning their hands to its subdual, to taming it rather than allowing it to shape them. At Wormhill is a drinking fountain in memory of James Brindley, almost illiterate, yet the greatest canal engineer of his time. He was born in a cottage at Tunslow where there still grows an ash known as Brindley's Tree. It began to grow through the floor of the cottage and in the end the cottage was sacrificed to the tree. This was a round won by Nature.

Of Brindley, Thomas Carlyle wrote:

'The English are a dumb people. They can do great acts but not describe them. Whatsoever of strength the man had in him will be written in the work he does. The rugged Brindley had little to say for himself. He has chained seas together. His ships do visibly float over valleys, and invisibly through the hearts of mountains; the Mersey and the Thames, the Humber and the Severn, have shaken hands.'

Erasmus Darwin, the physician, poet and philosopher, grandfather of Charles Darwin, lived in Derby for nearly twenty years and died at Breadsall Priory nearby. Sir Charles Fox, born at Derby, built the Crystal Palace and was inventor of the famous 'Fox's Patent Railway Switch'. His son, Sir Charles Fox, was responsible for the great bridges over the Victoria Falls, Sydney Harbour, the Mersey Tunnel and the Liverpool Overhead Railway. The designer of the Crystal Palace was a Derby man, too, Sir Joseph Paxton (1803–1865). Then there is Sir F. H. Royce, OBE, who in 1907 became joint founder, with the Hon. C. J. Rolls, of Rolls-Royce Ltd. Jedediah Strutt joined in 1770 with Richard Arkwright and together they started the cotton mills at Cromford, and Strutt's Derby Rib machine revolutionized the hosiery industry.

But my favourite Derbyshire character is one I came across only while I was researching to write this piece. I cannot resist introducing him because he is that figure familiar to every writer of fantasy, the truth stranger than the fiction. He is a man called Wright who lived in Tissington and had four sons whom he trained to be blacksmiths like himself. He then sent them out to found forges of their own, until in time about thirty of his descendants were carrying on the Wright tradition all over Derbyshire. One of them, Edward, had six sons, four of whom carried the family craft to Australia and

Canada. And even today descendants are to be found all over the world, not as smiths, but as its modern counterparts, oxy-acetylene and engineering experts. In my book *The Signposters* my imaginary family of the Flockshire Smiths (128 of them in all) seemed too far-fetched to be true to many people, possibly including myself. And yet it was true, after all, and I for one am glad of it.

If I were to set against the Derbyshire Wright a favourite Nottingham character, it would be a man who was born William Thompson but became the great prize fighter Bendigo, celebrated by Sir Arthur Conan Doyle as The Pride of Nottingham.

Later in his life he was converted, and became a popular preacher, managing to dovetail his religious and fighting urges in a practical and effective manner. There is a ditty about one of his prayer meetings that was being heckled by an unruly element in the front row:

'But the roughs they kept on chaffin' and the uproar it was such
That the preacher in the pulpit might be talking Double Dutch.
Till a working man he shouted out, a jumpin' to his feet
"Give us a lead, your reverence, and heave 'em in the street!"'
Then Bendy said, "Good Lord, since I first left my sinful ways,
Thou knowest that to thee alone I've given up my days.
But now dear Lord" (and here he laid his Bible on the shelf)
"I'll take with your permission just five minutes for myself!"'

There speaks your Midlander, a man of common sense and moderation. He is not made of the stuff of the saint or the fanatic. Even William Booth, founder of the Salvation Army, saw religion in fighting terms, and made himself a General. And Robin Hood, folk hero of Nottinghamshire, personifies idealism tempered by a robust streak of realism.

Perhaps this is why most of our local artists have moved away from the region, however widely they may have drawn on it for their art. The climate is not congenial. Lord Byron did not stay, nor Samuel Butler, D. H. Lawrence and Dame Laura Knight. We have no poets like John Clare and Wordsworth, or painters like Constable, whose roots lay in their region so deep that to pull them out would have meant death to their art. Artists are men of excess, and your Nottinghamshire man looks with a cold eye on extravagance of any kind, and expecially extravagance of feeling. He understands gumption better than inspiration.

But I can live and work and begin to put down roots here in north Nottinghamshire. It is a landscape where birches grow wild and the towers and wheels of pit-heads are always somewhere there on the horizon. It calls up images of old trees, black conical mountains, mossed stone. (Here, it seems, moss grows overnight). The winds blow bleak from the east over the bare Lincolnshire flats and make our nights stormy and our houses draughty. I think of them as white winds, cold and cleansing. The winters are bitter and we have more than our share of snow – but then we have more than our share of logs and coal, too. It is only a pleasure to be warm when it is cold outside.

LANCASHIRE HOTPOT

by Elfrida Vipont

'If ah see'd a cat fra Colne on my doorstep,' said the old man reflectively, 'ah'd ax it in an' gie it t'best i'th'ouse, ah would an' all. Aye, ah'd give it t'middle brick out o'chimley.'

The old man was homesick for his native town, yet few 'offcumd'uns' (as strangers are called in Colne) can see anything particularly delectable about the place. A typical Lancashire cotton town, it is perched on a ridge of the Pennines, its narrow streets of terraced houses slanting steeply and its old church rising proudly above the town on the crest of the hill. All 'reet Colners' call it 'bonny Colne on th'hill' and the nickname is an expression of their local pride. Proud of their town and its surroundings, they are also proud of their long history, for Colne is believed to have Roman origins. Roman soldiers are said to have camped on the prehistoric earthwork of Caster Cliff nearby and founded a settlement called Colunio.

To an outsider all the Lancashire cotton towns tend to look alike, but in fact they are fiercely independent and individualistic. They owe their existence to the damp climate, the Lancashire coalfields, the abundance of water and the facilities for transport. Dominated in their heyday by the great cotton mills, many of them began as little settlements of handloom weavers; Wycoller, near Colne, must have been just such a village, but there time has stood still. Its legendary history abounds in ghosts and phantoms – once a year a wild rider storms through the night and the ruined hall resounds with screams – but it owes its fame to the shy Brontë sisters who loved to walk there from Haworth, across the Yorkshire border, over the wild moors. Charlotte Brontë is believed to have had Wycoller Hall in mind when she described Ferndean Manor in *Jane Eyre*. The Brontë sisters have other, more tragic associations with Lancashire, for Charlotte and Emily were sent to a school at Cowan Bridge with their elder sisters, Maria and Elizabeth, who both died as a result of neglect. Charlotte's description of the school in *Jane Eyre* is so vivid and so utterly wretched that anybody reading it would expect Cowan Bridge to be a dismal, sinister place, whereas it is actually a pleasant village, with an old stone bridge over a trout stream which once a year is crowded with salmon coming up to spawn. The walk over the fields to the lovely old church at Tunstall (also in Lancashire) which Charlotte describes with such poignancy, is in reality a beautiful walk, even in the depths of winter, but not for delicate, half-starved, homesick little girls.

Time may have stood still at Wycoller, but many another settlement of handloom weavers was transformed out of all recognition at the time of the Industrial Revolution. Some kept up their old village traditions to within living memory – Great

Harwood its 'crier', Colne its 'mummers' who used to black their faces and rush through the houses on New Year's Eve, making a curious humming noise, and Bacup its morris dancers, who still come out from the nearby village of Britannia and dance through the streets on Easter Saturday. Other towns are associated with the great names of the Industrial Revolution – Bury with John Kay, inventor of the fly-shuttle, and Blackburn with James Hargreaves, inventor of the spinning-jenny. Samuel Crompton, inventor of the spinning mule, lived near Bolton, in an old house called Hall i' th' Wood, which was at that time split up into tenements. He received little benefit from his invention, which made fortunes for others, but long after his death another famous son of Bolton, Lord Leverhulme, restored the old house to something of its former glory and gave it to the town. It is now a folk museum and many of Crompton's relics are preserved there, including the little violin he made, which he used to play at the local theatre so that he might earn money to buy tools. Another manufacturing town, Rochdale, prides itself on being the birthplace of an idea which has spread throughout the world, for there, in 1844, a little group of working men now famous as the Rochdale Pioneers opened a small shop which was the beginning of the Co-operative Wholesale Society, better known to most of us as the Co-op.

Changes have come to the Lancashire cotton towns in recent times. Few Lancashire housewives put on their coarse 'brats' (aprons) and go down on their hands and knees to 'stone' their doorsteps and window sills, and even the pavements opposite their houses, with white or yellow donkey stone as they used to do, and Nelson is one of the very few places where you can still buy the genuine Lancashire oat cake, or haverbread, which used to be served in baskets and eaten instead of bread. Many of the cotton mills have been closed, or are used for other purposes, and no longer can you hear the thunderous sound of hundreds of clogs clattering over the stone 'setts' first thing in the morning. In the old days men and women workers alike wore heavy clogs with wooden soles strengthened with front 'cokers' and heel 'cokers' (clog-irons), and the clogger was an important member of the community who did a thriving trade. The women wore shawls over their heads and shoulders instead of coats and hats, and these would often be passed down from one generation to another. The Lancashire lass with her clogs and shawl has passed into legend, and much of the old Lancashire seems to have gone with her, but a good deal still remains.

The life of a Lancashire cotton town centred at one time round the mill. 'T'mill mun go on!' the mill owner would say with grim determination when apparently faced with ruin, for the closing of the mill was a disaster in such a close-knit community. Working expressions have passed into everyday speech: anybody from East Lancashire short of material to finish a job in the house or garden will still say that he or she is 'stopped for bobbins' or 'laikin' for weft' – 'laiking' comes from an old Norse word meaning to play. 'Tacklers' tales' are still an unending source of amusement. The tackler had a responsible job, keeping the looms in order, so his fellow workers got their own back by making a butt of him. Everybody knows about the tackler who asked for red oil to fill a red lamp, or who heaved the piano on to a wheelbarrow when he went to the music teacher for his first lesson, or who asked his mates to help him carry his henhouse. 'Wheer's eawr Sam?' they asked as they staggered up the hill. 'Ee, ah'm in 'ere carryin' t'perches!' called Sam from inside the henhouse.

Lancashire folk have an irrepressible sense of humour, and they seldom mind if the joke is against themselves. For example, the citizens of Wigan laugh as loudly as anybody else when comedians make fun of their town, though its history goes back to Roman times and it won its proud motto, *Ancient and Loyal*, from Charles II for its loyalty to the Stuarts. Nowadays people are more familiar with jokes about Wigan Pier than with stories of the town's romantic past, though the sad spirit of Mabel Bradshaw still performs its ghostly penance, barefoot, to Mab's Cross. Mabel believed her husband to have been killed in the Crusades and so married again, but later he returned and demanded vengeance. The interloping second husband was killed, and she, though she had acted in all innocence, was condemned to do penance for the rest of her life by walking once a week from Haigh Hall to Wigan Cross, barefoot and dressed in white, with a lighted candle in her hand. And so, they say, she does to this day. Perhaps jokes about Wigan Pier are pleasanter to live with.

Certainly Lancashire folk live happily with jokes of all kinds, even if they are macabre ones, like the story of the sick man who smelt a good smell of cooking from downstairs.

'Eh, ah could just fancy a bit o' that 'am!' he said.

'Nay, lad,' protested his wife. 'Ah canna cut into yon. It's for thi funeral!'

As for Mr and Mrs Ramsbottom, and the lion who ate up eawr Albert 'and 'im in 'is Sunday clothes too', only to disgorge him later and lose them the insurance money; they have passed into the folk lore of the county.

Eawr Albert's little mishap occurred in Blackpool, the most famous of Lancashire's many seaside resorts. In the old days the manufacturing towns used to empty themselves in turn into Blackpool during 'Wakes Week', the annual holiday when all the mills closed down. Nowadays, like everybody else, Lancashire folk like to vary their holiday haunts, but Blackpool is still a favourite resort. 'When ah dee,' said an old man to his wife, 'ah'd like thee to bury me i'Blackpool.' The old lady hesitated. 'Ee, lad, that'll tak a lot o'brass,' she said. ''Appen we'd best bury thee 'ere and see 'ow tha settles.'

Nonconformity is strong in Lancashire, in spite of its unfavourable reception in earlier days. Lancashire folk tolerated 't'owd religion' (Roman Catholicism) in spite of the persecuting authorities, so that in country districts the Roman Catholic tradition has been unbroken through the centuries. 'New-fangled ideas', however, tended to set everybody by the ears. George Fox was mobbed in the streets of Lancaster and Ulverston, and on the shore at Walney Island, and John Wesley and his supporters were similarly treated at Roughlee and Colne and Padiham. Nevertheless, Quakerism and Methodism and other branches of Nonconformity took firm root.

In the cotton towns 'Anniversary Sunday' is an important date in the calendar. Each chapel celebrates the anniversary of its foundation with special services and the engagement of a special preacher, and these occasions are often referred to locally as 'Sermons'. A certain chapel once engaged a woman preacher for the first time. Finding on her arrival that she was expected to conduct the service as well as to preach, she looked through the order of service carefully.

'What does this mean?' she inquired, pointing to a large question mark opposite the word anthem.

Nobody seemed to know, so the choir master was sent for.

'What's this 'ere, Fred?' he was asked.

Fred drew himself up and looked severely at the company. 'If theer's a good turn-up, theer'll be a hanthem,' he said. 'And if not – there *wean't*!'

Anniversary Sunday is often marked by a Sunday School procession through the town, but the greatest place for religious processions is Manchester, where the 'Whitsuntide Walks' are famous. At one time the centre of the city would be blocked on successive days by crowds of children carrying flowers, youths carrying banners, and clergy marching with their congregations to the music of brass bands. Little or no business could be done in Manchester during Whit Week, but protests went unheeded. To some this was an act of Christian witness, to others a splash of beauty and colour which brought a certain radiance into the town. The 'Walks' now only take place in a modified form, but they are still one of the sights of Manchester.

Manchester, dismissed by many as a drab, commercially-minded place, is actually one of the most exciting cities in the world. Mancunians accept, or even invent, innumerable jibes against their city – 'The quickest way out of Manchester is to get drunk!' they say – but they remain quietly confident in their unshaken belief that what Manchester does today, England will do tomorrow. Whatever the rest of the country may say, and whatever its official title may be, many of them still refer to their great newspaper as *The* Manchester *Guardian*, and cherish the story of the worthy man engaged in an extempore prayer who said, 'Oh Lord, as thou has doubtless seen in *The Manchester Guardian* . . .' Older people look back to the days when the famous editor, C. P. Scott, could be seen cycling down to his office from his home in the suburbs; for that matter, they still remember the great philosopher, Sir Samuel Alexander, cycling down to the University, with his long beard flying in the wind and an expression on his face which showed that his mind was occupied with higher things than the traffic.

Manchester has pioneered in many fields, industry and trade, scientific research, canals, railways and air travel, and many of her ideas have been regarded in the early stages as 'plain daft'. Her determination against all reason to become a great port, with direct access to the sea, led to the construction of the Manchester Ship Canal, which is an extraordinary feat of engineering. The Barton Aqueduct, where the Bridgewater Canal is taken over the Ship Canal on a swing bridge, is one of the sights of Lancashire. Later on, the city was so early in providing a civic airport that many denounced the scheme as crazy and grudged the expense involved in promoting this adventure in cloud cuckoo land.

Manchester's latest pioneering experiment is an educational one. The old Bluecoat School, Chetham's Hospital, has been developed as a co-educational school for musically gifted children. The medieval buildings once housed a college for priests attached to the parish church, now the cathedral. Humphrey Chetham planned to turn them into a school for poor boys, and for centuries the boys in their long blue gowns and flat Tudor hats were a familiar sight in the heart of Manchester. Now the city, which already has in the Hallé one of of the finest orchestras in the world, has embarked upon this imaginative experiment which is attracting musical children from all over the country.

Lancashire is a musical county and this shows itself in all manner of ways, from handbell ringers in Silverdale to symphony concerts in Manchester and Liverpool, and from pop groups and folk singers in town and country to brass band contests at Belle Vue. Belle Vue is a zoo and amusement park in Manchester. Within living memory it was a little privately-owned zoo with a few merry-go-rounds, and a boating lake, and an open-air dance floor where the mill folk would dance on summer evenings, for the most part lads with lads, and girls with girls. If you were lucky, you might meet the proprietor, Mr Jennison, and see him talking with the animals in their cages, and animals talking back to him.

The relationship between the sister cities, Manchester and Liverpool, is rather like a north-country family relationship, secretly loving but outwardly critical. There may have been a touch of envy in Manchester's old insistence on the terms 'Manchester men' and 'Liverpool gentlemen', for Manchester has nothing like the Pier Head, where you may stand, whipped by the keen wind, and feel yourself linked up with far countries overseas. Both cities suffered cruelly in the blitzes of the Second World War – Liverpool probably as badly as any city in the country – and both have responded proudly with re-building schemes. Many of the worst slums have been swept away, and it remains to be seen whether the warm neighbourliness which brightened life in those dismal areas has survived.

Neighbourliness is a characteristic of Lancashire towns, large and small, and if this quality has a patron saint, then Liverpool may lay claim to her in Kitty Wilkinson. Kitty was a washerwoman in a poor street in Liverpool and her husband, Thomas, was a porter in the Rathbones' warehouse – the Rathbone family of Liverpool has been active in all kinds of social reform. Kitty was loved and trusted as a good neighbour, always ready to befriend young people, or visit the sick, or look after orphaned children. When a cholera epidemic broke out and terrified people were dying like flies, she fought it with the only weapons she had, soap and water, compassion and elbow-grease. Soon she inspired courage in other women, who offered to help her with the endless task of washing the infected linen, and then the Rathbones stepped in and helped to provide a proper washhouse, which eventually became the first public washhouse in Liverpool. Long after cholera had been stamped out in England, Kitty Wilkinson's name was remembered, and she is now commemorated in the 'Noble Women' window in Liverpool's Anglican cathedral.

Another Lancashire good neighbour was Mary Higgs of Oldham, who was determined on two things: to make Oldham beautiful and to improve the condition of the tramps. She invented the phrase 'beautiful Oldham', and worked hard to make it a true description, in spite of ridicule. And because nobody seemed to be interested in the tramps, especially the women tramps, she went 'on the road' herself, in ragged clothes and an old shawl, and then told people about the conditions in the casual wards and the lodging-houses from her own experience. In her old age, she was honoured with an OBE. She went to Buckingham Palace in her best clothes but she told her friends, with a twinkle in her eye, that she had been sorely tempted to turn up in her lodging-house outfit! People who loved her used to call her 'Mother Mary', and they long remembered the lesson of her life, which was surely that if you want to make a dream come true, you must do something about it yourself.

Like Mary Higgs, Michael Graham saw the possibility of creating beauty in unlikely places. He left his native Lancashire as a young man, but after a distinguished career as a marine scientist, he decided to return to the northwest. Naturally he was expected to choose the Lake District for his retirement, but during one of his journeys northward, he passed through the blighted region of the slag heaps and suddenly felt challenged by them. He and his wife settled first in Eccles, near Manchester, and then in Horwich, near Bolton, and soon he worked out his own methods for reclaiming the derelict land. He bought an Arab mare and rode her slowly round his first slag heap, treading a firm track and then sowing seed in the hoof marks. The local children were attracted, first by curiosity, and then by Michael Graham's friendliness, until one after another, they clamoured to be allowed to help. So many flocked to his aid that he became known as the Pied Piper of Lancashire. He developed his work on scientific lines until what had been an isolated effort became a recognized movement, sponsored by the authorities. By the time he died, in 1972, the tips he had tackled, at first single-handed, were covered with grass and trees and gay with wild flowers, an abiding monument to a man of faith and vision and practical commonsense.

In spite of tips and coal mines, and factories and mill chimneys, the huddled towns of south and east Lancashire never seem to be far away from the countryside, especially in the east, where so many of them are dominated by Pendle Hill. Pendle Hill is famous as the haunt of the Lancashire Witches, whose story is told in Harrison Ainsworth's *Lancashire Witches* and in Robert Neill's *Mist over Pendle*. It is a solitary hill, rising from the plain like some humpbacked, crouching, prehistoric beast, and its sinister reputation is traditional. Even today there are still folk living on the slopes of Pendle who ignore the doctor's advice to sleep with their bedroom windows open in hot weather, because of the risk that witches, or boggarts, or demons, or the Devil himself may fly in.

The Devil seems always to have been a familiar presence in Lancashire, especially in the Pendle area. He is said to have paid a visit to Crawshawbooth, near Rawtenstall, when some lads were playing a forbidden game of football on a Sunday.

Not recognizing him, they invited him to join in their game and found him to be a better player than even the best of them. At last he gave a stupendous kick, and the lads cheered wildly as the ball rose high into the air. On and on it soared, until suddenly they realized that it was disappearing into the sky. Terrified, they turned to their strange companion, only to catch a glimpse of cloven hoofs and forked tail as he vanished in a blinding flash of flame. The smell of sulphur, they say, lingered in Crawshawbooth for days.

On the whole, boggarts seem to be easier to deal with than devils or demons. Some boggarts are like 'Lob-lie-by-the-fire' and will do your work in farmhouse and dairy if you know how to treat them. On the other hand, they can be as mischievous as Puck, in which case you long to be rid of them, like the family who decided to move house because their boggart would give them no peace. Their furniture was stacked on a cart, and their neighbours were helping them to shove in the last oddments, when suddenly a shrill little voice from inside the milk churn said, 'We's flittin' – aye – we's flittin'!'

The farmer shook his head and began to unpack his household goods again. There was no point in 'flitting' if the boggart was determined to 'flit' too!

In spite of its strange reputation, Pendle Hill was the place where George Fox, founder of the Quakers, saw his famous vision, after he had climbed to the top 'with much ado, it was so steep'. As he looked to the north and west he 'saw Lancashire sea; and there atop of the hill I was moved to sound the day of the Lord; and the Lord let me see a-top of the hill in what places he had a great people to be gathered'. You may climb Pendle Hill a score of times and see no view, let alone a vision, but on a clear day you can stand on its bare summit with the curlews and peewits crying in the wind, and look out over mile upon mile of rolling fell country, rising higher and higher, with the Lake District stretched across the horizon to the north and 'Lancashire sea' to the west.

Not far from Pendle Hill, in the valley of the Calder, lie the ruins of Whalley Abbey and the great church of Whalley, with its Saxon crosses and Roman relics and the lovely choir stalls taken from the abbey church. But older than the great abbey and older than the church is the Christian tradition of this place, for here, early in the seventh century, St Paulinus, friend of St Augustine, preached to the people and baptized his converts in the Calder.

Below Whalley the Calder flows down to join the Ribble, which winds through rich farmland, with old halls and farms along its banks. At one point, where there used to be a ford, two important Roman roads met, one the road northward from the fort at Mamucium (Manchester) to Petriana (Stanwix, near Carlisle, the headquarters of the legions guarding Hadrian's Wall) and the other going eastward across the Pennines to Eboracum (York). Here the Romans built a great fort called Brematanacum, far bigger than the one at Mamucium because obviously Brematanacum was a more important place. Time has now passed it by, and the sleepy little town of Ribchester, which stands on its site above a lovely, winding stretch of the Ribble, where in former days the Roman galleys would sail in and out of the harbour, does not show much obvious evidence of its former greatness. You have to look closely before you realize that the stone pillars supporting the porch of the White Bull, with its grotesque wooden figure of a bull leering above them, are Roman, that those supporting the gallery in the old church are also Roman, and that countless fragments in the church and in the surrounding houses have come from the old Roman town. Treasures turn up casually from time to time; an object kicked about by an idle boy on the river bank in the late eighteenth century turned out to be a Roman ceremonial helmet, which is now in the British Museum. There is a curious atmosphere about the place, as if something in its spirit must have died when the Romans left and – judging by the traces of fire in the granaries – the settlement went up in flames.

The Ribble flows on towards Preston, past Salmesbury

where the magnificent old hall is now the headquarters of the Lancashire branch of the Society for the Preservation of Rural England. Whether the Society has preserved the Salmesbury ghost is uncertain; a white lady, still mourning the death of her lover, is said to appear there at night, and even to startle passing motorists on the A59.

Preston is the market town for a wide agricultural area and it is also an increasingly busy port. A great event is Preston Guild, celebrated once every twenty years with processions and pageantry; 'once every Preston Guild' is a local saying meaning 'once every blue moon'. Preston and neighbouring Walton-le-Dale are two places where you can still sometimes buy 'carlings' (black peas) and learn the legend of Carling Sunday, which is the Sunday before Palm Sunday. This festival is still observed in Cumberland, especially near the Solway, where most of the public houses will produce a dish of carlings on the appointed day. The story, found in several other places in the north of England, is that in a time of famine a boat sailed into port with a cargo of carlings, and the starving people were able to eat their fill. One theory is that the story was invented to explain the ceremonial eating of carlings, which probably goes back to pagan days. Similarly the custom of egg-rolling on Easter Monday, observed by thousands of Preston children at Avenham Park, is believed to have a pagan origin. Egg-rolling still takes place in many of the Lancashire villages, Aughton and Downham and St Michaels-on-Wyre among them, though in others it has died out.

Richard Arkwright, pioneer of the cotton industry, was born in Preston and set up his spinning machine there until the handloom weavers drove him away to Bolton. The Temperance Movement started in Preston, where the word 'teetotal' was coined by a stammering enthusiast, and Preston was also the birthplace of the poet, Francis Thompson. Proud Preston, as the town is called in Lancashire, honoured her famous son when the citizens raised £700 rather than see one of his manuscripts leave the country.

North and west of Preston stretches a great plain of rich agricultural land, bounded by the sea on one hand and the rising fells on the other. Up on the fells to the north, above Bleasdale, a prehistoric circle similar to Woodhenge, in Wiltshire, has been found. The wooden posts were still in position, though they had to be moved to Preston Museum for preservation and concrete blocks fixed in their place. The wooden circle of Bleasdale is the only one of its kind in the north of England, though there are stone circles at Yealand Conyers, near Carnforth, and Birkrigg Common, near Ulverston.

You can still pick up stone axes and bone arrow heads round the Yealand villages, and this may be because they stand on a high ridge (Yealand comes from the Anglo-Saxon 'geah-land' meaning high-land) and all around them would probably be swamp in prehistoric times. A group from Lancaster University has discovered traces of a lake village, like the one at Glastonbury, on the 'Mosses' near Yealand Redmayne. The Royal Society for the Protection of Birds has established a bird reserve here, and when it was set up, the Yealand villagers sighed with relief, for they had long known that rare birds, including bitterns, were breeding on the Mosses, but they had never dared to make this known for fear of egg-stealers and other vandals. During the Second World War there was an evacuation school in Yealand Conyers. Most of the children came from north country towns, a few from the London area, and some from the Continent, but soon it was noticed that they were all keeping up the seasonal cycle of children's games. At one time they would be playing hopscotch, at another marbles, and at another 'chuckstones' or 'bobs and kibbers'. Then the skipping ropes would appear, and all the children would be skipping to the rhythm of skipping chants which almost every child seemed to know.

The Yealand villages lie to the north of Carnforth, which used to be an important railway junction and now has a fascinating railway museum called Steam Town. Close by is Warton, the home of the Washington family; the church tower was built by the Washingtons, and on Independence Day the American flag flies proudly from its flag-pole over the grey roofs of the village. Yealand and Warton have local sayings which you seldom hear elsewhere. Yealanders describe a brisk gale as 'an idle wind' (because it goes straight through you instead of going round you), and Warton folk call a wiry little woman 'a nurry lile body' and a difficult child 'a lile nowt-o'-clock nuisance'.

The market town for all this area is Lancaster, with its castle rising above the Lune. The site has been fortified since Roman days to guard the river and the road to the north. Protestants, Catholics and Quakers alike have suffered in Lancaster Castle. The Lancashire Witches were chained for months in the icy underground dungeons before they were taken out to be hanged on Gallows Hill; the eyeless heads of courageous, tortured priests were exposed from its grim towers; and it was there, in the Great Hall, that the dauntless Margaret Fell defied her judge when he sentenced her to be outlawed: 'Although I am out of the King's protection, I am not out of the protection of the Almighty God,' she said.

The Lune is a famous salmon river. At Lancaster it is tidal, and in the days when Lancaster had two railway stations, it used to be possible for the guards on the trains crossing the railway bridge to report to the staff at Green Ayre Station if they had seen a stranded salmon on the muddy sandbanks at low tide. The best parts of the valley of the Lune are in Yorkshire and Westmorland, but Lancashire has the famous Crook of Lune near Caton, and there are some lovely villages on the Lancashire side of the border, including Ireby, on the fringe of the pot-holing country, and Aughton, high above the river, where the famous Pudding Festival has recently been revived.

There is something solid and satisfactory about celebrating a pudding. Indeed, there is something solid and satisfactory about Lancashire food in general, from Lancashire hotpot, tripe and onions and Bury black puddings to Eccles cakes and Grimsargh cakes and Ormskirk gingerbread. Lancashire hot-pot is not to be confused with potato pie, though this too is a popular dish. A potato pie supper at a ploughing, hedging and ditching competition is something to be remembered, especially when the singing starts afterwards. Hotpot is made with neck end of mutton, potatoes and onions in alternate layers, and well seasoned; the top layer is always potatoes, well-browned in the oven, and you eat it with pickled onions, or beetroot, or pickled red-cabbage. Another Lancashire delicacy is the genuine Lancashire cheese, strong-flavoured, with a crumbly texture, and quite unlike the pallid, tasteless stuff which passes for Lancashire in other parts of the country. Genuine Lancashire cheese is too good to be exported.

North of Lancaster begins the country of the piel towers, which were built in the days of the border raids from Scotland. Some of them were single one-storey affairs, just sufficient to provide shelter for the peasants and their stock during a raid. Normally these were snatch-and-grab affrays, so that strong walls and good bolts were all that was needed. Some of the towers were more elaborate, with an upper storey reached by a winding staircase from the ground floor, which was used for the stock. Furness Abbey maintained a big piel tower on an island near the mouth of Morecambe Bay. It was more like a fully-fledged castle than a piel tower, and Lambert Simnel and his supporters used it as a base when they were disputing Henry VII's claim to throne. After England and Scotland had been united under one king, the border raids gradually ceased and the piel towers were allowed to moulder away, though a few were enlarged into manor houses for the gentry. Lesser folk in the villages now began to build stone houses instead of wattle and daub huts; there had been no point in building good houses to be burnt by the raiders from across the border.

At the mouth of the Lune, beyond Lancaster, there is a strange tidal country, with miles of sandbanks, and roads which disappear under the water at high tide. On the southern shore, at the tip of the estuary, are the ruins of Cockersand

Abbey, battered by the wind and pillaged by men. Only the chapter house survives, with a few crumbling walls and fallen stones; nothing more is left of what was once a great abbey, except for the choir stalls from the abbey church, which are now in Lancaster Priory. Other Lancashire abbeys have fared better. Cartmel still has its magnificent priory church, and Furness Abbey, which is near the great ship-building town of Barrow, still has its string of lovely, roofless, rose-coloured buildings in the Valley of the Deadly Nightshade which, so tradition says, lost its poison in the presence of the holy monks. Across the estuary from Cockersand is Sunderland Point, which can only be reached at low tide, and there the first cargo of cotton to reach Lancashire was landed. A curious tree grows there known as the Cotton Tree, and not far away is the grave of poor Sambo, who died of a broken heart when he thought his master had deserted him in a foreign land.

At Lancaster you are not far from the borders of Westmorland and Yorkshire, but there is still a large area of the county beyond, called Furness*, which is completely cut off from the rest of the country by the wide sweep of Morecambe Bay. The bay is tidal, so that the great seaside resort of Morecambe, near Lancaster, is deserted by the sea twice in the twenty-four hours. On the other hand, it has surely the finest view of any seaside resort, with a whole chain of the Lakeland hills rising above the lower fells on the other side of the bay. Not far from Morecambe is Heysham, where the steamers set out on the night crossing to Belfast. Legend has it that St Patrick himself landed there from Armagh and built the little oratory which bears his name, up on the crest of the headland which juts out into the sea. Be that as it may, there is little doubt that it was built by Celtic missionaries and it was regarded for centuries as a holy place.

Another great saint is traditionally connected with Morecambe Bay. It is said that after the faithful monks had fled from Lindisfarne before the heathen raiders, carrying with them

* Now in administrative area of Cumbria.

the coffin of St Cuthbert, they wandered for years through the north of England, unable to find a safe place where they might lay the saint to rest once more. In the course of their wanderings, they passed through Furness and crossed the wild sands of Morecambe Bay, and it is said that wherever they passed, they left behind them an atmosphere of peace and holiness which can be sensed to this day. It is also said that wherever the coffin rested, a church was built, and certainly there are churches dedicated to St Cuthbert on both sides of the Bay, one at Aldingham and one at Nether Kellet.

The Bay is dangerous to cross because of the swift-flowing tides which come sweeping up the river channels, and because of the quicksands, which shift about so that you can never be sure exactly where they are. In the old days, it took a long time to go inland to the nearest bridge over the Kent, and so there was a regular route marked out across the sands. So many people were drowned, or lost in the quicksands, that the great abbeys near the Bay maintained guides who collected all the travellers together at low tide and led them across in safety. After Henry VIII dissolved the monasteries, the guides were still needed, so they were maintained by the Duchy of Lancaster, as they are to this day. People still like to cross the sands on foot, but it is never safe to go without a guide, and even so, people can get into difficulties if they disobey him. An old guide once lectured a group before they attempted to cross the Kent channel, which is the most dangerous part of the crossing when the river is running deep and the current is swift.

'Look oop all the time,' he said. 'If ye look dahn, ye'll get dizzy. Theer were a big chap in a party yesterday who wouldn't tak' no notice, so 'e looks dahn, and afore 'e knew wheer 'e were, 'e were laupin' abaht like a gurt stag.'

People who 'laup abaht' can easily be drowned, so 'heads up!' is the rule when there is a strong current to pull you under. This is not a bad rule for life in general, as the writer of Psalm 121 knew full well.

The channel of the Kent is on the northern side of the Bay,

near Grange-over-Sands, and this is the best place to see the bore, when the tide comes up the channel in a wall of water in rough weather, though on a calm day it can be nothing more than a ripple. Within living memory the fishermen at Grange-over-Sands used to count their catches in the old Celtic numerals – 'yan, tyan, tethera, methera, pimp, sethera, lethera, hovera, dovera, dick'. These were also used by the Lakeland shepherds for counting their sheep.

Much of the southern part of the Lake District is in Lancashire. Coniston (home of John Ruskin and later of Arthur Ransome), Esthwaite, the western shore of Windermere, and the heights of Coniston Old Man, Wetherlam and the Dunnerdale Fells. The Duddon Valley is the northern boundary of the county, and up at the head of it, on Wrynose Pass, is the Three Shires Stone, where Lancashire, Westmorland and Cumberland meet.

Now that climbing and pot-holing have become popular sports, people in south and east Lancashire are used to seeing young people setting off by road or rail with climbing and caving kit, but not so long ago they were thought to be 'daft'. A young man once presented himself at the ticket office of the local station, complete with rucksack and climbing boots. The old railway clerk looked at him very severely.

'Windermere return, please,' said the youth cheerfully, and the old man sighed.

'Eh, lad,' he said at last. 'Asta nivver thowt, if God 'ad meant them 'ills to be walked on, 'e'd 'a put 'em lower dahn.'

In the heart of Lancashire Lakeland is Hawkshead, where young William Wordsworth went to school, and where you can still see his name carved boldly on his desk, in the little grammar school near the old church. But the shop where they used to bake Hawkshead pasties has gone, though it used to be well worth walking or cycling into Hawkshead to buy one. They were encased in rich puff pastry made with butter, and filled with currants and candied peel and syrup and brown sugar. Doubtless the village baker made them in Beatrix

Potter's day, though Ribby, the little cat in *The Pie and the Patty Pan*, only bought muffins when she went to his shop with her basket. Beatrix Potter lived at Sawrey, at the other end of Esthwaite, and her house is now a museum, where you can see so many things which you can recognize from the illustrations in the Peter Rabbit books that you almost expect to see Peter Rabbit and Tom Kitten and Jemima Puddleduck as well.

Beatrix Potter's illustrations show a Lancashire remote from manufacturing towns and coal mines, yet this was once an industrial area, with copper mines at Coniston and forges in the Furness valleys. The abbots of Furness held the rights for smelting ore by means of charcoal in the Furness area, and these passed to local landowners at the Dissolution. In the seventeenth century Force Forge, in the Rusland Valley, was owned by the Fell family of Swarthmoor Hall, near Ulverston. The ore was mined near Dalton-in-Furness and carried by pack-horses by way of Lowick Bridge and Nibthwaite to Force Forge, where there was plenty of coppice to supply charcoal, and a swiftly-flowing stream for water power to work the bellows. For some years Force Forge was managed by one of the Fell sisters, Sarah Fell, though it was very unusual in those days for a woman to undertake such a job.

In the quiet Rusland valley one can well imagine a future time when Michael Graham's grassy slag-heaps may look down on yet another 'green and pleasant land'. If so, Lancashire folk will be to the fore in shaping a new world, for they have shown that they can survive changes without losing their essential qualities – their Lancashire grit, and their Lancashire inventiveness, and their Lancashire sense of humour. And surely, whatever happens in the future, they will never lose their passionate love for their county.

'If ah see'd a cat fra Colne on my doorstep,' said the old man, 'ah'd ax it in and gie it t'best i'th'ouse, ah would an' all.'

So would anyone Lancashire-bred, in any part of the world, for any cat from any place in Lancashire. So would I. 'Ah'd gie it t'middle brick out o'chimley!'

SUGGESTIONS FOR FURTHER READING

Land's End by Jacynth Hope-Simpson

Baker, Denys Val, *Adventures Before Fifty* (John Barker, 1969)
Causley, Charles, *Underneath the Water* (Macmillan, 1968)
Du Maurier, Daphne, *Jamaica Inn* (Gollancz, 1947)
Du Maurier, Daphne, *Vanishing Cornwall* (Gollancz, 1967)
Quiller-Couch, Arthur, *Castle Dor* (Dent, 1962)
Rowse, A. L., *A Cornish Anthology* (Macmillan, 1968)
Rowse, A. L., *A Cornish Childhood* (Cape, 1962)
Tangye, Derek, *A Gull on the Roof* (Michael Joseph, 1961)
Treneer, Anne, *School House in the Wind* (Cape, 1944)

The Rolling, Windy Acres and the Powerful, Timeless Sea by Pauline Clarke

Barrett, W. H., *Tales from the Fens* (Routledge, 1963)
Brooke, Justin & Edith, *Suffolk Prospect* (Faber & Faber, 1963)
Clark, R. Rainbird, *East Anglia* (S.R. Pub., 1971)
Ketton-Cremer, R. W., *Norfolk Assemblies* (Faber & Faber, 1957)
Ketton-Cremer, R. W., *Norfolk Portraits* (Faber & Faber, 1948)
Porter, Enid, *Cambridgeshire Customs & Folklore* (Routledge, 1969)
Warrington, (Editor), *The Paston Letters* (Dent, Everyman's Library, 1924)
Woodforde, James, *The Diary of a Country Parson* (O.U.P. World Classics, 1947)

A Ghost of London by Leon Garfield

Besant, Walter, *London in the Eighteenth Century* (Chatto & Windus, 1892)
George, *London Life in the Eighteenth Century* (Penguin, 1968)
Phillips, Hugh, *Mid-Georgian London* (Collins, 1964)
Pottle, F. (Editor), *Boswell's London Journal* (Heinemann, 1973)
Thornbury, Walter, *Old and New London* (Cassell, 1872)
Ward, Ned, *The London Spy* (Folio Society, 1955)

An Ancient Place by Penelope Lively

Beresford, M. W., *History on the Ground* (Methuen, 1971)
Beresford, M. W., *The Lost Villages of England* (Lutterworth Press, 1954)
Emery, F. V., *The Making of the English Landscape: Oxfordshire* (Hodder & Stoughton, 1973)
Hoskins, W. G., *Field Work in Local History* (Faber & Faber, 1967)
Hoskins, W. G., *The Making of the English Landscape* (Penguin, 1970)

I Was Born in the Midlands by Helen Cresswell

Hutchinson, Lucy, *Memoirs of Colonel Hutchinson* (Dent, 1965)
Knight, Laura, *The Magic of a Line* (Kimber, 1965)
Lawrence, D. H., *Sons and Lovers* (Heinemann, 1969)
Lawrence, D. H., *The White Peacock* (Heinemann, 1962)
Mee, Arthur, *Derbyshire* (Hodder & Stoughton, 1969)
Mee, Arthur, *Nottinghamshire* (Hodder & Stoughton, 1970)
Pevsner, Nikolaus, *The Buildings of England, Nottinghamshire* (Penguin, 1969)
Roberts, Cecil, *The Growing Boy* (Hodder & Stoughton, 1967)
Roberts, Cecil, *The Years of Promise* (Hodder & Stoughton, 1968)
Trease, Geoffrey, *Nottingham* (Macmillan, 1970)

Lancashire Hotpot by Elfrida Vipont

Bagley, J. J., *A History of Lancashire* (Darwen Finlayson Ltd., 1967)
Collins, Herbert G., *Lancashire, Plain and Seaboard* (Dent, 1953)
Corbridge, Sylvia L., *It's an Old Lancashire Custom* (Guardian Press, Preston, 1964)
Cuming Walter, J., *Charm of Lancashire* (Black, 1920)
Lofthouse, Jessica, *Portrait of Lancashire* (Robert Hale, 1967)
Lofthouse, Jessica, *The Curious Traveller – Lancashire to Lakeland* (Robert Hale, 1972)
Mee, Arthur, *The King's England* (Hodder & Stoughton, 1936)
Spartina, *Looking at North Lancashire* (Dalesman Publishing Company, 1971)
Spartina, *Looking at Central Lancashire* (Dalesman Publishing Company, 1971)
Spartina, *Looking at South Lancashire* (Dalesman Publishing Company, 1971)